AF693562

Inside The Sentence

Inside the Sentence:

The Complete Practice Guide for Sentencing Consultants

"Justice isn't complete until it's understood."

By David R. Carrillo, MBA

Inside the Sentence: The Complete Practice Guide for Sentencing Consultants

This publication is intended for educational and professional purposes. It is not a substitute for legal advice or professional counsel. Readers are encouraged to consult with licensed attorneys or other qualified professionals regarding individual cases or legal matters.

Published by:

David R. Carrillo Consulting, LLC
Denver, Colorado, USA
www.davidrcarrilloconsulting.com

Library of Congress Control Number: 2026910928
ISBN (Paperback): 979-8-9999256-3-3
ISBN (eBook): 979-8-9999256-4-0

Printed in the United States of America
Design and interior layout by David R. Carrillo

For everyone who deserved to understand before they signed.

Table of Contents

Acknowledgments

Every page of this work was built on the shoulders of people who believed in transformation, not as a slogan, but as a practice.

First and foremost: to my **sister**, Christie Broney, who carried my name when I could not; and to every person who stood by me during three decades behind the wall, this is our victory.

To the men and women I met during my incarceration, those who trusted me to translate the system's language into human words, you were my first clients, my first classroom, and my first reason to build this work.

To the **attorneys**, **educators**, and **justice professionals** who invited me into your classrooms, offices, and conferences, thank you for giving this profession a voice.

To Jamie Ray and my colleagues at the **Korey Wise Innocence Project** and the **Legislation on the Inside** team, your support and trust in me have helped me to move with confidence.

To my colleagues and students at **Adams State University** and **Red Rocks Community College**, your curiosity and courage fuel my commitment to teaching.

To **Canary Impact** for the additional support they provided to help make this book possible.

To Governor Jared Polis, for the clemency that made freedom possible; and to the community of advocates who never stopped believing that people can change.

Finally, to **every attorney and client who seeks understanding, and every professional committed to integrity, not just outcomes**:

May this book serve as a bridge between law and life, a reminder that justice is not complete until it is understood.

David R. Carrillo, MBA
Sentencing Consultant, Educator, and Author
Denver, Colorado

Purpose of This Manual

This book is more than a guide. It's a blueprint for an emerging profession.

It is designed to:

- Define the consultant's role and ethical boundaries;
- Teach step-by-step consultation methods;
- Provide tools and templates for documentation;
- Clarify the legal foundation under *Strickland*, *Frye*, *Lafler*, and *Padilla*;
- Offer business models and educational pathways for professional growth; and
- Inspire a new standard of informed justice through structure, empathy, and integrity.

Each chapter builds on the next, from theory to practice, from practice to profession, from profession to reform.

Who This Book Is For

- **Consultants** seeking structure, ethics, and credibility in their work.
- **Attorneys** who want to enhance client comprehension and reduce the risk of post-conviction claims.
- **Students and educators** studying sentencing, ethics, and correctional policy.
- **Advocates and reformers** working to humanize justice through education and communication.

It speaks equally to practitioners and visionaries, those who see justice not as a static system, but as a living process that must be constantly refined.

How to Use This Book

Each chapter includes:

- **Legal Foundations:** The case law and constitutional standards that define consultation.
- **Professional Practice:** Tools, checklists, and methods for real-world implementation.
- **Ethical Insight:** Discussion of confidentiality, neutrality, and professionalism.
- **Case Studies:** Illustrations of consultation in action.

And the appendix includes:

- **Templates and Forms:** Ready-to-use materials for building your own system.

Read it as a manual, teach it as a curriculum, or use it as a training reference or educational program.

Disclaimer:

The author of this manual is not a licensed attorney. This manual provides general information on professional practice in sentencing consultation. It is not intended to constitute legal advice or to substitute for consultation with a licensed attorney or any other licensed professional. The author and publisher disclaim any liability resulting from the use or misuse of the material contained herein.

About the Author

David R. Carrillo, MBA, is an educator, consultant, and national advocate for informed justice and higher education in prison. After spending more than 30 years in the Colorado Department of Corrections, much of it in high-security facilities, Carrillo rebuilt his life through education, service, and purpose.

While incarcerated, he earned multiple academic degrees and became the **first incarcerated person in the United States to be hired as a college instructor**, teaching *Introduction to Business* and *Macroeconomics* for Adams State University inside a correctional facility.

Since his release in 2024, Carrillo has founded **David R. Carrillo Consulting, LLC**, which offers sentencing consultation, plea-bargain analysis, collateral-consequence education, and justice-centered training.

He also works with the Korey Wise Innocence Project's ***Legislation Inside*** program at the **University of Colorado Boulder**. He served as an adjunct instructor for **Adams State University** and teaches programs inside prisons for **Red Rocks Community College**, and has spoken at national events, including the **U.S. Department of**

Education's Office of Correctional Education, Jobs for the Future/Horizons Conference, The National Conference on Higher Education in Prison, and the **National Reentry Workforce Conference**.

Carrillo's mission is to ensure that every client and every attorney understands the sentence before it begins. His philosophy is simple:

Justice is not complete until it's understood.

A Note on Authorship

This book was born from lived experience, learned, and earned through decades inside and outside the walls of the justice system.

It reflects a simple but revolutionary belief: that understanding is as essential to justice as representation, and with true understanding comes a peace of mind in the client that allows for focus on rehabilitation.

My path from incarceration to consultant and educator taught me one truth: knowledge, when structured with empathy and ethics, becomes liberation.

This manual is dedicated to those who believe the same.

Foreword

When I first began working with people returning home from prison, I repeatedly heard two narratives. The first: "I should never have taken that deal—I could have won at trial or received a lighter sentence." The second: "I should never have gone to trial—the plea wasn't great, but I would have served far less time."

Though these statements are opposites, they share the same underlying truth: *I did not fully understand my options when I had to decide.*

As attorneys, we are often asked to take on roles far beyond legal representation. We are expected to be counselors, social workers, therapists, financial advisors, and more. Despite our best intentions, we frequently fall short in areas outside our training.

That is why David's work is so important. Being an effective attorney means knowing how to use the right resources, and this is one every defendant should have. People deserve to understand the court process and to make informed decisions about their futures.

Equally important, this kind of support allows public defenders and other criminal defense attorneys to focus more fully on their legal advocacy, knowing their clients are receiving guidance in other critical areas.

I am excited to see more attorneys adopt this model and to see more professionals like David welcomed into this space, where their specialized and much-needed skills can make a meaningful difference.

Jamie Ray
Attorney at Law and co-founder of Legislation Inside

Preface: Bridging Law and Life

Justice is more than a verdict. It's understanding.

Every day in courtrooms across the country, defendants make the most consequential decision of their lives, to accept or reject a plea bargain, without truly understanding what that decision means.

They hear the words, but not the weight. They see the years, but not the realities.

And too often, those misunderstandings echo through decades of incarceration, regret, grievances, lawsuits, and appeals.

The Constitution guarantees the right to counsel. But the Constitution only guarantees minimal effort to satisfy that right, and that is where the sentencing consultant steps in.

This manual was written to fill that gap.

The Origin of a Profession

The field of sentencing consultation grew from the lived experience of those who have walked through the justice system and understand, firsthand, the difference between what's said and what's understood.

What began as informal guidance is evolving into a structured, ethical, and evidence-based practice supporting attorneys and clients alike.

Today, sentencing consultants should be prepared to act as interpreters of consequence, helping attorneys meet constitutional duties, protecting clients from confusion, and reinforcing the integrity of every plea and sentence.

Chapter 1: The Origins and Role of Sentencing Consultation

Introduction: The Missing Link in Criminal Defense

In the American criminal justice system, over ninety-four percent of criminal convictions result from plea bargains rather than jury trials. This reality makes the plea negotiation stage one of the most critical moments in a defendant's life. Yet, far too often, defendants accept plea offers without truly understanding their full implications. Miscommunication, legal jargon, and the emotional weight of incarceration can leave individuals confused, fearful, and ill-prepared to make informed decisions.

Additionally, after realizing the plea bargain didn't fully explain exactly what an individual will be facing often leaves individuals confused, angry, and disenfranchised. These individuals then struggle to focus on rehabilitation and often focus a lot of time on filing claims of ineffective assistance of counsel, legal malpractice, or grievances against their attorneys. They expend a lot of energy, time, and resources fighting an uphill battle to find justice from a perceived injustice.

Sentencing consultants fill this gap. They provide clarity, context, and practical insight that allows both attorneys and their clients to navigate plea and sentencing decisions with confidence. Allowing the client a full understanding of what they are getting into will, in turn, provide peace of mind that will allow the client to focus on rehabilitation and success beyond their criminal justice experience.

A sentencing consultant is not a lawyer; rather, they are an educator, interpreter, and strategist helping transform complex legal and institutional information into a clear, actionable understanding.

For attorneys, working with a sentencing consultant enhances communication, reduces misunderstandings, and can help ensure compliance with constitutional obligations regarding client advisement. For defendants, consultation offers empowerment and understanding during a process that often feels mechanical and dehumanizing.

The Evolution of Sentencing Consultation

Historically, defense counsel handled all aspects of plea negotiations and sentencing discussions alone. However, as criminal justice systems became more complex, introducing layered sentencing grids, collateral consequences, parole restrictions, and specialized facilities, attorneys are increasingly recognizing the need for specialized assistance.

Sentencing consultation emerged organically from this evolution. It developed at the intersection of **legal advocacy**, **corrections expertise**, and **human understanding**. Individuals with lived experience in prisons, parole, and the legal process began to offer information and guidance to attorneys and defendants on what a sentence to prison may look like. What to expect when going to prison, how to carry oneself in such a new environment, and how to avoid some of the major pitfalls of the prison culture.

Sentencing consultation is now taking its next step in its evolution. Sentencing consultants now bring with them their lived experience, academic training, and professional credibility, offering even greater structured guidance to attorneys and defendants. Providing information surrounding the true consequences of accepting a particular plea.

These consultants bridge two worlds: they understand **how sentences work in theory** and **how they unfold in practice**. For example, how does the acceptance of a particular plea impact classification upon entering the Department of Corrections, which in turn impacts earned (good) time? Their work supplements the legal process by ensuring that clients not only ***hear*** their options but ***comprehend*** the realities that follow each one.

The Constitutional Foundation: The Duty to Inform

At the heart of effective sentencing consultation lies the constitutional guarantee of effective counsel under the **Sixth Amendment**. The United States Supreme Court has repeatedly affirmed that defendants have a right to be fully and accurately informed about plea offers and their consequences.

Strickland v. Washington, 466 U.S. 668 (1984)

In *Strickland*, the Court established the two-pronged test for *ineffective assistance of counsel*:

1. **Deficient performance**; whether counsel's performance fell below an objective standard of reasonableness; and
2. **Prejudice**: Did the deficient performance result in harm? That is, but for the deficient performance, the result of the proceedings would have been different.

Strickland's framework has become the foundation for all claims involving the duty of counsel to advise clients accurately, including during the plea-bargaining stage.

Consulting Implication:

Sentencing consultants reinforce the *Strickland* standard by helping attorneys ensure that defendants fully understand plea offers, sentencing ranges, corrections classifications, earned (good) time, and other collateral impacts. This not only supports the constitutional duty to inform but also helps prevent future grievances, claims of ineffective assistance, or legal malpractice suits.

The Modern Standard: Frye and Lafler

The Supreme Court expanded the *Strickland* framework in two landmark 2012 cases: ***Missouri v. Frye*** and ***Lafler v. Cooper***. Together, they cemented plea negotiations as a critical stage of criminal proceedings requiring competent, informed legal guidance.

Missouri v. Frye, 566 U.S. 134 (2012)

In *Frye*, defense counsel failed to inform the defendant of a formal plea offer before it expired. The Court held that such an omission violated the Sixth Amendment, emphasizing that the duty to communicate plea offers is essential to effective representation.

Key Holding:

Defense counsel has a duty to communicate formal plea offers to the defendant before they expire. Failure to do so constitutes deficient performance under *Strickland.*

Consulting Application:

A sentencing consultant ensures that when an offer is presented, it is fully explained, not just legally, but practically. The consultant helps the defendant understand:

- The exact sentence exposure under the plea.
- The alternative if the case proceeds to trial, and
- The real-world impact on incarceration, parole (probation or supervised release), and family life.

Through this process, the consultant supports attorneys in meeting their *Frye* obligations and ensures defendants make informed choices.

Lafler v. Cooper, 566 U.S. 156 (2012)

In *Lafler*, the defendant rejected a plea offer based on his attorney's mistaken advice regarding sentencing exposure. After conviction at trial, he received a much harsher sentence. The Supreme Court held that incorrect legal advice during plea bargaining could also amount to *ineffective assistance of counsel.*

Key Holding:

Deficient legal advice that causes a defendant to reject a favorable plea offer may constitute ineffective assistance under the Sixth Amendment.

Consulting Application:

A consultant's role is to prevent this very outcome by offering clarity, realism, and context. Consultants help defendants understand:

- What a plea *actually means* in terms of daily life inside.
- How parole eligibility, good time (or earned time), and program access affect sentence duration.
- The social, emotional, and familial consequences of the decision.
- And, most importantly, help make clear the consequences of rejecting a fair and reasonable plea.

Consultants do not replace attorneys; they empower them. By supplementing counsel's legal advice with practical insight, they help clients make truly informed decisions and avoid the misunderstanding that led to *Lafler*'s reversal.

The Ethical Imperative

Beyond constitutional requirements, sentencing consultation serves a deeper ethical purpose: ensuring that justice is *understood.* The legal system can easily become transactional, treating pleas as administrative necessities rather than moral choices. But to the person standing before the court, every decision carries the weight of years, relationships, and identity.

By helping defendants comprehend what is at stake, consultants restore dignity to the process. They reaffirm that informed consent must be more than a signature; it must be an act of genuine understanding. This is both a professional and a moral duty.

The Consulting Mindset

An effective sentencing consultant blends three disciplines:

1. **Legal Acumen:** A working understanding of criminal procedure, plea negotiation, and sentencing structures.
2. **Institutional Insight:** Practical knowledge of prison systems, classification, programming requirements, application of earned (good) time, and post-sentence realities.
3. **Human Understanding:** The ability to interpret emotional, cultural, and behavioral cues to communicate effectively with clients under stress.

The consultant's role is not adversarial; it is educational. The best consultants bring humility, empathy, and precision. They know that clients often nod in agreement without comprehension. The goal is not to lecture but to illuminate, to give them power in a seemingly powerless situation through information.

Defining the Consultant's Role

Sentencing consultants:

- Clarify the implications of plea bargains, probation, parole, and corrections.
- Prepare clients emotionally for sentencing and incarceration.
- Support attorneys by translating institutional knowledge into usable insights.
- Create written summaries that strengthen documentation of informed consent.

They do not:

- Offer legal advice or interpret statutes beyond factual explanation.
- Replace the role of defense counsel.
- Promise or guarantee outcomes.

Instead, they act as interpreters of consequence, helping all parties see the lived realities behind the legal language.

The Boundary That Protects Everyone: Scope of Practice in Sentencing Consultation

The sentencing consultant occupies a specific and bounded role in the criminal justice system. That role is valuable precisely because it is defined. A consultant who stays within scope provides something attorneys cannot provide alone and does so in a way that strengthens the attorney's representation rather than complicating it. A consultant who exceeds that scope creates legal risk for themselves, professional risk for the attorney, and potential harm to the client they are trying to serve.

This section establishes the scope of practice for sentencing consultation. It defines what the role includes, what it explicitly excludes, when a consultant must decline a request, and how to handle the situations where those lines are tested. This framework applies across every chapter of this manual and every consultation a practitioner conducts.

What the Role Includes

A sentencing consultant's authorized scope covers four functions, all of which exist in support of the attorney-client relationship and the constitutional duty to inform.

Function	What It Looks Like in Practice
Explain	Translate legal terms, sentencing structures, correctional processes, release mechanisms, and collateral consequences into plain language that the client can understand and restate.
Clarify	Identify and correct misunderstandings about the plea, the sentence, the pathway, or what incarceration or supervision will actually involve.
Document	Create written records of the consultation, intake forms, comprehension acknowledgments, collateral consequence worksheets, and consultation summaries that support the attorney's file and demonstrate informed consent.
Refer	Recognize when a client's circumstances require expertise outside the consultant's scope, such as immigration law, mental health evaluation, veterans' benefits, and forensic psychology, and ensure the attorney knows that referral is needed.

What the Role Excludes

The following actions fall outside the authorized scope of sentencing consultation in every circumstance. They constitute the unauthorized practice of law (UPL) or a related professional boundary violation, and engaging in them creates liability for the consultant and potentially for the attorney who retained them.

Outside Scope—Never Do This	Within Scope—Do This Instead
Advise a client on whether to accept or reject a plea offer.	Explain the plea terms, the release mechanism, and the collateral consequences, then confirm comprehension. The decision belongs to the client.
Interpret how a statute or case applies to this specific client's situation.	Explain what the statute or case generally means, and direct case-specific questions to the attorney.
Negotiate directly with a prosecutor, court staff, or any party outside the defense team.	Communicate only through and with the supervising attorney. All external contact flows through counsel.
Draft, review, or modify plea agreements, motions, or any legal document.	Review documents to understand them for explanation purposes. Leave drafting and legal review to the attorney.
Represent the client in any hearing, proceeding, or legal correspondence.	Attend proceedings only in an observer or support capacity, and only with explicit attorney authorization.
Provide clinical mental health assessment, treatment, or diagnosis.	Observe and adapt communication when a client presents with difficulty. Flag concerns to the attorney. Refer to qualified specialists.
Provide immigration legal analysis for non-citizen clients.	Identify that the client is a non-citizen, flag immigration exposure to

	the attorney immediately, and ensure immigration counsel is engaged.
Provide veterans' benefits analysis or VA claims guidance.	Identify veteran status, flag VA benefit collateral consequence concerns to the attorney, and refer to a VA-accredited specialist.

When to Decline a Consultation

Professional scope is not only about what happens during a consultation, but it is also about whether to accept a consultation in the first place. There are three situations in which a sentencing consultant must decline engagement, either entirely or until the conditions that triggered the concern are resolved.

Situation 1: The Request Falls Outside Authorized Scope

Scenario:

An attorney asks the consultant to explain to the client why they should accept the plea offer, or to tell the client that going to trial is too risky. The attorney wants the consultant to make the case for the plea.

Why this is outside scope:

This is strategic legal advice. The consultant's role is to ensure the client understands the plea, not to advocate for or against it. Taking on this request crosses directly into the attorney's function and creates UPL exposure.

How to respond:

"I can explain everything about what the plea means and what the client would be agreeing to, conditions, release timeline, collateral consequences. The decision itself, and any advice about whether to take it, has to come from you as counsel. That's where my role stops."

Situation 2: The Consultation Cannot Proceed With Integrity

Scenario:

A client arrives to a consultation visibly intoxicated, in acute mental health crisis, or so distressed that meaningful participation is not possible. Or a client is being pressured in real time by a family member sitting in the room who answers questions on the client's behalf.

Why this is outside scope:

Informed consent requires that the client is actually capable of receiving and processing information in that moment. Proceeding with a consultation and collecting signatures when the client cannot meaningfully participate produces a document that does not reflect genuine comprehension. That document protects no one.

How to respond:

"I need to reschedule this session. [To the attorney:] I don't believe the client is in a state to meaningfully participate today. I want to make sure the documentation we produce actually reflects their understanding, and we're not there yet. Can we set a new time?"

Situation 3: A Conflict of Interest Exists

Scenario:

The consultant has a prior personal relationship with the client, a financial stake in the outcome of the case, or a relationship with another party in the proceedings, a victim, a co-defendant, or a witness that could compromise impartiality.

Why this is outside scope:

Consultation integrity depends on the consultant having no interest in the outcome other than accurate comprehension. A conflict, even a perceived one, undermines that integrity and could expose the attorney to claims that the consultation was not impartial.

How to respond:

"I need to disclose something to you before we proceed. [Describe the relationship or conflict.] I think you should decide whether you want me involved, given that, and I'll defer entirely to your judgment. If you'd prefer I refer you to another consultant, I'm happy to do that."

The Language of Boundaries—Scripts for Common Situations

The situations below arise regularly in practice. Each one involves a request or moment that tests the scope boundary. The script provided is not mandatory language; it is a model for how to hold the boundary professionally, without being rigid, dismissive, or defensive.

When a client asks for your opinion on whether to take the plea:

Client: *"What would you do if you were me? Should I take it?"*

Consultant: *"I hear you, that's the hardest question in the room. But that's exactly the decision I can't make for you or push you toward. My job is to make sure you understand everything so that when you do decide, you're deciding with the full picture. What's the part you're most uncertain about?"*

When a client discloses something that requires a specialist:

Client: *"I was in the military. Does that change anything?"*

Consultant: *"Yes, it very well might. I'm not the right person to analyze all of it, but veteran status can affect your options here significantly. I'm going to flag this for your attorney right now. Before we go any further, we need to make sure that piece is being looked at properly."*

When someone asks you to do something you cannot do:

Attorney: *"Can you just review the plea agreement and tell me if anything looks off legally?"*

> **Consultant:** *"I can read through it to understand it well enough to explain it to the client, that's within what I do. But reviewing it for legal adequacy is your territory, not mine. I don't want to create any confusion about where my role ends and yours begins. Happy to go through it together if that would help."*

Why the Boundary Protects Everyone

It protects the client. A client who receives strategic legal advice from a non-attorney has received something the non-attorney is not qualified to give. If that advice is wrong, or if it appears to have influenced the client's decision in ways that later become relevant in post-conviction proceedings, the client has been harmed, not helped.

It protects the attorney. An attorney who uses a consultant who operates outside the scope may face questions about the validity of the consultation, the integrity of the documented comprehension, and whether the consultant's involvement created any unauthorized practice of law problem. A consultant who stays within scope is an asset. One who doesn't is a liability.

It protects the consultant. UPL is not a hypothetical concern. State bar authorities and criminal courts take unauthorized practice of law seriously. A consultant who provides legal advice, interprets case strategy, or holds themselves out as capable of legal analysis they are not qualified to provide is exposed to professional and potentially legal consequences.

It protects the field. Sentencing consultation is an emerging profession. Its credibility depends on practitioners who understand what it is and what it is not. Every consultant who stays within scope and performs that role with rigor makes it easier for the next consultant to be taken seriously by the next attorney. Every consultant who oversteps makes that harder for everyone.

Consulting Implication: Read this section before your first consultation. Return to it whenever a situation arises that feels uncertain. The boundary is not a limitation on the value you provide; it is the reason the value you provide is trustworthy. An attorney who knows exactly what you will and will not do is an attorney who can use you with confidence. That confidence is the foundation of every professional relationship this work requires.

Case in Point: When Consultation Prevents Crisis

Consider a defendant offered a 15-year plea deal with the possibility of parole after seven. Without context, that offer may appear lenient or harsh depending on perception. The attorney explains the statutory language, but the defendant's understanding remains surface-level.

A sentencing consultant breaks down the real meaning:

- How good (earned) time is actually applied;
- The projected release date with good (earned) time;
- The type or level of facility likely assigned;
- Availability, access, and the need to participate in rehabilitative programs, which can impact good (earned) time;
- The impact on family visits, work release, and reentry options.

Armed with this information, the client can make a decision aligned with both legal advice and lived reality. This consultation not only supports the attorney's ethical duty under *Frye* and *Lafler* but also prevents future post-conviction litigation alleging ineffective assistance, grievances, or even potential legal malpractice claims.

Conclusion: Consultation as a Bridge to Informed Justice

Sentencing consultation is more than a profession; it is a bridge between law and life. It exists at the intersection of constitutional law, ethics, and human experience. As the criminal justice system continues to evolve, the demand for transparency and comprehension will only grow.

By helping attorneys meet their legal obligations and defendants understand their decisions, sentencing consultants become vital actors in advancing a more equitable system. They embody the principle that *justice is not only done, but it must also be understood.*

Key Takeaways

- Sentencing consultation supports the *Sixth Amendment* right to effective assistance of counsel.
- *Strickland v. Washington*, *Missouri v. Frye*, and *Lafler v. Cooper* form the legal backbone for consulting relevance.
- Consultants provide non-legal but critical clarity that bridges communication gaps between counsel and client.
- Effective consultation promotes ethical practice, reduces litigation risk, and restores dignity to the plea process.

Chapter 2: Lived Experience as Expertise

Introduction: Turning Time Served into Knowledge Earned

In the courtroom, expertise is often defined by degrees, credentials, and bar admissions. Yet, within the criminal justice system, there exists another kind of expertise, one that cannot be earned through textbooks or traditional study. It comes from having lived the system from the inside out.

Those who have experienced incarceration firsthand possess a perspective that few others can match. They understand not just the statutes and sentencing ranges, but the *human* consequences of those numbers. The way a ten-year sentence feels in lived time, how facility placement determines opportunity or despair, and what it truly means to reenter society after years of confinement.

This chapter explores how lived experience, when properly developed and framed, becomes a professional asset in the world of sentencing consultation. It also addresses the ethical and practical steps needed to transform personal history into a credible, professional service.

From Surviving the System to Understanding It

The difference between surviving incarceration and understanding incarceration is reflection. Many individuals endure the experience;

fewer analyze it. The process of turning trauma into teaching requires introspection, education, and purpose.

As a consultant, your lived experience becomes valuable when it is filtered through discipline and transformed into structured knowledge. Attorneys and clients do not seek stories; they seek insight. The challenge, then, is to translate firsthand experience into a clear, applicable understanding that advances justice.

This begins with a mindset shift: seeing your past not as a liability, but as a credential earned through endurance, growth, and study. Experience alone is not enough; what makes it powerful is the ability to *interpret* and *communicate* that experience to help others make better decisions.

Building Credibility from Experience

Professional credibility is built at the intersection of **authenticity** and **competence**. Lived experience grants authenticity; education, discipline, and professionalism add competence.

To build credibility as a sentencing consultant with justice-impacted experience, three elements are essential:

1. **Educational Foundation:** Supplement personal knowledge with formal education in law (paralegal studies) and maybe business or behavioral studies. Degrees or certifications demonstrate commitment to professionalism and reassure attorneys of your analytical capability.
2. **Professional Presentation:** Maintain a standard of dress, communication, and documentation consistent with the legal environment. Every consultation, email, and report should

reflect a tone of precision and respect. You are not reliving your past; you are redefining it.

3. **Ethical Clarity:** Transparency about your background is important, but so is discretion. Share your story strategically, only when it serves to strengthen trust or illustrate a principle. The goal is not self-promotion; it's transformation.

Reflection Sidebar:

"The credibility I have today was not built on my degrees alone; it was built on my ability to turn my past into purpose. Experience gave me insight, education gave me language, and integrity gave me authority."

The Unique Value of Insider Knowledge

Lived experience in the criminal justice system provides access to a realm of understanding that cannot be simulated or fully researched. It gives consultants a deep awareness of the *unwritten realities* of incarceration that influence sentencing outcomes but rarely appear in statutes or plea paperwork.

These include:

- **Institutional Culture:** Understanding prison hierarchies, safety dynamics, and behavioral expectations that influence where and how a defendant will serve time.
- **Classification Systems:** Knowledge of how facility placement, security levels, programming requirements, and case factors affect the quality of incarceration.
- **Program Access and Earned (Good) Time:** Insight into how sentence structure, behavior credits, and program

participation can meaningfully reduce or increase actual time served.

- **Post-Sentence Realities:** Awareness of parole board expectations, reentry challenges, and the true weight of collateral consequences.

This perspective allows consultants to provide attorneys and clients with information that is both *accurate* and *contextual*, bridging the legal framework with lived reality.

Humanizing the Process

Lived experience brings more than procedural insight; it brings empathy. Consultants who have experienced incarceration firsthand can communicate with clients in ways attorneys often cannot. They understand the language of fear, shame, and hopelessness that accompanies criminal prosecution.

For many defendants, particularly those from marginalized backgrounds, the criminal justice process feels alienating. The consultant becomes a translator, not only of legal terms but of human emotion. By normalizing the fear and confusion clients experience, consultants create an environment where learning and understanding can take place.

When a client feels seen and heard, they become more receptive to their attorney's advice. Thus, consultants with lived experience can indirectly improve attorney-client relationships and case outcomes.

Ethics and Boundaries in Sharing Experience

While personal experience is powerful, it must be handled with care. Consultants should avoid making themselves the focus of the consultation. The goal is to use experience as a bridge, not a spotlight.

Best Practices:

- **Share selectively:** Use personal stories only when they illustrate a point or clarify a process relevant to the client's situation.
- **Avoid glamorization:** Recounting past violence or criminal conduct in detail can be counterproductive.
- **Maintain professionalism:** Always return the focus to the client's needs and legal circumstances.
- **Disclose appropriately:** Be transparent with attorneys about your background, but let your professionalism define your reputation.

Ethical consulting means leading with empathy, not ego. Your credibility comes from how you conduct yourself now, not from what you survived before.

Case Study: Turning Experience into Insight

Scenario:

A defense attorney represents a young client facing a plea deal for a serious felony. The client's family is panicking. The attorney can explain sentencing ranges and statutory terms, but struggles to help the client understand what the plea *really means.*

Consultant's Role:

Drawing from lived experience, the consultant explains:

- The likely facility placement based on the offense and behavior.
- The programs that are required based on the offense or behavior, and programs not required but could be beneficial.
- How good time and earned time credits function in practice.
- The day-to-day environment of incarceration at different custody levels.
- How education, behavior, and participation in programs can affect release eligibility.

The client gains perspective. The family understands the difference between 10 years on paper and 6 years in practice. The attorney now has a calmer, more informed client capable of making a reasoned decision.

This is how lived experience, when applied professionally, transforms fear into understanding and misunderstanding into clarity.

Professional Integration: Education Meets Experience

Experience becomes expertise when it is merged with education and structured methodology. Many consultants with lived experience strengthen their practice through:

- **Paralegal or legal studies education** (for procedural fluency).
- **Business or entrepreneurship education** (for operations and branding).

- **Behavioral science or counseling coursework** (for communication and emotional intelligence).
- **Ethics and professional development training** (for credibility with attorneys and institutions).

The more structured the consultant's approach, the more seamlessly their lived experience integrates into the professional legal environment.

Consulting Insight Box:

The more you study the system that once confined you, the more effectively you can teach others how to navigate it.

The Consultant's Transformation Narrative

Each consultant's journey represents a microcosm of reform. A person once defined by a sentence now becomes a guide to understanding sentencing. This transformation is both personal and professional; it signals a redefinition of expertise itself.

By embracing your past as a source of wisdom rather than shame, you become part of a growing movement to professionalize lived experience. You model for attorneys what it looks like to merge compassion with precision, and you demonstrate to clients that knowledge and redemption can coexist.

Conclusion: The Power of Credibility Born from Experience

Lived experience, when combined with education and ethical conduct, forms one of the most powerful foundations for sentencing consultation. It provides the human context missing from many legal interactions and transforms the consultation process from a transaction into a transformation.

The effective consultant stands at the intersection of law, humanity, and experience, bridging the system that once defined them to the profession they now define.

Through disciplined professionalism, structured knowledge, and empathy rooted in authenticity, lived experience becomes not a reminder of where you've been, but a testament to how far you've come.

Key Takeaways

- Lived experience becomes professional expertise when structured through reflection, education, and discipline.
- Credibility arises from the balance of authenticity (your story) and competence (your professionalism).
- Consultants with lived experience add value by humanizing the process, clarifying incarceration realities, and improving attorney-client understanding.
- Ethical boundaries are essential; thus, experience should inform, not overshadow, the consultation.

Chapter 3: Understanding the Three Pathways of Sentencing

Introduction: The Architecture of a Sentence

When a defendant stands before the court, the decision being made is not simply prison or freedom. It is entry into one of three distinct, structured pathways of state authority. Each pathway reshapes liberty in a different way. Each imposes conditions. Each carries consequences that extend well beyond the moment of sentencing.

Yet in practice, these pathways are frequently confused by defendants, by families, and sometimes even by counsel. A client sentenced to community corrections may believe they are "basically on probation." A family relieved their loved one avoided prison may not understand that the halfway house carries its own search authority and its own potential path toward deeper incarceration. A defendant accepting a plea to a county jail sentence may not grasp that jail, though shorter in duration, is structurally identical to prison in terms of the authority it exercises over daily life.

This chapter establishes the foundational framework that every sentencing consultation must begin with the three pathways of sentencing which are Institutional Confinement, Structured Community Placement, and Conditional Community Supervision. Understanding where a sentence falls and what that means in concrete, lived terms, is the first obligation of any consultant working with attorneys and their clients. The duty to inform discussed in Chapter 4 cannot be fulfilled without it.

The Three Pathways Model is the foundational framework of this manual. It establishes that every sentence leads to one of three distinct pathways of state authority, Institutional Confinement, Structured Community Placement, or Conditional Community Supervision, each with a different relationship between the individual and the system that holds power over them. Identifying the correct pathway is the first obligation of every sentencing consultation.

THE THREE PATHWAYS MODEL

A Framework for Sentencing Consultation

Every sentence imposed in a criminal proceeding leads to one of three distinct pathways of state authority. The pathway determines the nature of custody, the structure of daily life, the consequences of noncompliance, and the mechanism of release. Understanding which pathway a sentence represents, and ensuring that the client understands it in concrete, operational terms, is the first obligation of every sentencing consultation.

The Three Pathways Model provides a consistent framework for that obligation. It is not a spectrum from harsh to lenient. Each pathway represents a fundamentally different relationship between the individual and the authority the state holds over them. Confusion between pathways is one of the most common sources of uninformed pleas, post-conviction grievances, and preventable violations.

The model applies across all fifty states and the federal system. Terminology varies by jurisdiction. Structure does not.

THE THREE PATHWAYS MODEL

Quick-Reference Diagram for Consultants, Attorneys, and Clients

PATHWAY ONE Institutional Confinement	PATHWAY TWO Structured Community Placement	PATHWAY THREE Conditional Community Supervision
LIBERTY STATUS		
Liberty Removed Physical custody transferred to institution	**Liberty Partially Restored** Present in community; institutional authority remains	**Liberty Conditionally Retained** Present in community; subject to court supervision
AUTHORITY STRUCTURE		
Correctional institution controls daily life, movement, and conduct	Facility or agency holds immediate authority, including administrative removal	Court and probation officer hold supervisory authority through conditions
COMMON NAMES BY JURISDICTION		
County jail · Local jail State prison · DOC Federal BOP · Detention center Correctional facility	Community corrections Halfway house · Work-release Residential Reentry Center (RRC) Transition center · CBCF	Probation · Supervised probation Formal probation · Community supervision Suspended sentence Conditional discharge · ISP

KEY CONDITIONS		
Classification & housing level Institutional rules & discipline Program participation Visitation restrictions Release mechanism (parole / mandatory)	Residential confinement Curfews · Employment requirement Drug testing · Program participation Search authority Administrative termination	Regular officer reporting Drug testing Treatment / programming Travel restrictions Financial obligations
CONSEQUENCE OF VIOLATION		
Disciplinary action Loss of earned time · Classification increase · Segregation	**Administrative termination** Removal without court hearing · Return to incarceration	**Revocation hearing** May result in suspended sentence imposed · Incarceration
MOST COMMON CLIENT MISUNDERSTANDING		
"Jail is not as serious as prison" Both are Pathway One. The pathway is the same, only duration and facility differ.	"Community corrections is basically probation" It is not. Staff can return a client to incarceration without a judge.	"Probation means I'm free" It does not. Conditions are real. Violations have real consequences.
CONSULTANT'S FIRST QUESTION IN EVERY CASE		
"Which pathway is this sentence, and does the client understand what that means?"		

1. Pathway One: Institutional Confinement

Institutional confinement is any sentence in which liberty is physically removed, and authority over the individual is transferred to a correctional institution. It is the pathway most people picture when they hear the word "sentence," but it is often understood only in part.

The terminology varies significantly by jurisdiction. This pathway may be called county jail, local jail, detention center, regional jail authority, state prison, Department of Corrections, state penitentiary, Federal Bureau of Prisons, correctional institution, or correctional facility. The name matters far less than the structure. Whether the sentence is six months in a county jail or twenty years in a state prison, the defining feature is the same: liberty is removed, and daily life is controlled by the institution.

Explaining institutional confinement to a client requires covering each of the following elements without exception:

- The length of confinement and how the sentence will actually be served
- Credit for time already served in pretrial detention
- Good time or earned time eligibility, including how it is calculated and what can forfeit it
- Classification and housing level, which determine facility type, programming access, and daily conditions
- Institutional rules governing conduct, visitation, communication, and movement
- Program availability, including educational, vocational, and treatment offerings
- The release mechanisms, such as parole, mandatory release, or sentence completion, and what each requires

One of the most common gaps in consultation involves county jail sentences. Because they are shorter in duration, jail is frequently treated as a lesser concern by defendants, by families, and sometimes by counsel. It should not be. A jail sentence carries restricted movement, institutional discipline, limited programming, limited visitation, and immediate loss of autonomy. A client who enters a thirty-day jail sentence without understanding its structure is no better prepared than one who enters prison without that understanding. Short sentences still require informed comprehension.

Consulting Implication: When a client is facing any form of institutional confinement, the consultant's role is to translate the abstract into the concrete. The sentence is not just a number. It is a classification process, a facility, a daily routine, a set of rules, and a release mechanism. Clients who understand this before they enter are better equipped to navigate it, and attorneys who document that understanding are better protected against post-conviction claims.

2. Pathway Two: Structured Community Placement

Structured community placement occupies the space between incarceration and probation. It is institutional authority operating within the community rather than inside a facility, and that distinction is the source of the most persistent confusion consultants encounter.

This pathway goes by many names. Depending on jurisdiction, it may be called community corrections, residential community corrections, halfway house, work-release program, residential reentry center (RRC), community-based correctional facility (CBCF), community custody, community placement, community residential facility, alternative custody program, intensive residential supervision, transition center, diversion center, intermediate sanction facility, probation detention center, or community control. As with institutional confinement, the name is secondary to the structure.

In structured community placement, liberty is partially restored; the individual is physically present in the community, but authority remains immediate and institutional. This placement typically includes some combination of the following:

- Residential confinement, meaning a required residence at a designated facility
- Curfews governing when and where the individual may travel
- Employment requirements, including mandatory job searches and income reporting
- Drug testing, often conducted without advance notice
- Mandatory program participation, such as cognitive behavioral programming or treatment
- Search authority, allowing staff to search the individual's person and belongings at will
- Financial contributions toward the cost of placement
- Administrative termination authority, meaning staff can remove a participant without a court hearing

That last point, administrative termination, is frequently misunderstood and underexplained. A participant in community corrections can be removed and returned to jail based on a rule violation. The standard of proof is not the same as a criminal hearing. The speed of removal, depending on jurisdiction, can be immediate. Clients who do not understand this dynamic may approach community placement with the casual confidence of someone on probation, and pay a severe price for that misunderstanding.

Consulting Implication: Consultants must be unambiguous with clients about the nature of structured community placement. It is not probation. It is not freedom. It is a correctional environment that happens to exist in the community rather than behind walls. The rules are real, the authority is real, and the path back to incarceration can be shorter and faster than most clients anticipate. A thorough consultation on this pathway should include a specific conversation about the facility's rules, the termination process, and what behaviors typically trigger removal.

3. Pathway Three: Conditional Community Supervision

Conditional community supervision is a court-imposed sentence of conditional liberty. Unlike structured community placement, the individual in this pathway is not confined to any facility. Unlike institutional confinement, their physical liberty is not removed. But liberty is not unconditional; it is held subject to a set of requirements, any significant violation of which can result in revocation and incarceration.

This pathway is most commonly called probation, but it appears under other names as well: supervised probation, formal probation, community supervision, community control, suspended sentence, conditional discharge, or intensive supervised probation (ISP). The structure is the same regardless of the label.

Probation commonly requires some or all of the following:

- Regular reporting to a probation officer, in person or by phone
- Drug testing, on a schedule or randomly
- Participation in treatment, counseling, or educational programming
- Prior approval for travel outside the jurisdiction
- Maintained employment or active job search
- Financial obligations, including supervision fees, fines, restitution, and court costs
- Behavioral compliance, including no new arrests and no contact with specified individuals

Violation of these conditions does not automatically result in incarceration, but it can. A probation revocation hearing, triggered by a violation report from the probation officer, may result in the suspension being imposed, meaning the original sentence that was held in abeyance now becomes a term of imprisonment. Clients who enter probation thinking of it as freedom are unprepared for this reality.

Consulting Implication: Probation is not the absence of punishment. It is structured supervision under court authority, and clients who treat it as freedom often become clients facing revocation. A consultant's role here is to ensure the client understands not just the conditions of their probation but the practical consequences of each one, what reporting actually looks like, what happens if they miss an appointment, what 'no new arrests' means in terms of daily behavior, and how fees accumulate. The client who walks into probation informed is the client most likely to complete it successfully.

4. Why This Clarification Matters

The three-pathway framework is not academic. It has direct, practical consequences for every consultation, every plea discussion, and every sentencing recommendation a consultant touches.

When a client is sentenced to county jail, they are not entering a lesser form of the first pathway. They are in the same pathway as someone, for example, who is sentenced to a state prison, differentiated only by duration and facility type. The authority structure is the same. The loss of autonomy is the same. The need for informed understanding before entry is the same.

When a client is sentenced to community corrections, they are not on probation. They are in structured community placement under correctional authority, with a short, administrative path back to jail and even prison depending on the terms of the original plea bargain. Treating this placement like probation is a mistake that ends careers and adds years to sentences.

When a client is sentenced to probation, they are not free. They are conditionally free, under supervision, subject to a set of requirements that, if violated, collapse that conditional liberty back into incarceration.

Clarity about these distinctions protects defendants from making uninformed decisions. It protects attorneys from post-conviction claims rooted in inadequate communication. And it protects the integrity of the plea itself, because a plea accepted without understanding the pathway it leads to is not truly an informed plea. The duty to inform that runs through the Supreme Court's framework in Strickland, Frye, Lafler, and Padilla (see Chapter 4) depends entirely on this foundational clarity.

When Sentences Move Across Pathways: Split Sentences and Sequential Structures

The Three Pathways Model describes three distinct forms of state authority. Most sentences live entirely within one pathway for their duration. But some sentences are deliberately structured to move from one pathway to another, and a consultant who does not address this creates a comprehension gap as significant as confusing pathways in the first place.

The most common multi-pathway structure is the split sentence. A split sentence imposes a term of Pathway One, Institutional Confinement, followed immediately by a term of Pathway Three, Conditional Community Supervision, as part of a single sentencing order. The client serves the incarceration component, is released, and transitions directly into supervised probation. Both pathways are active components of the same sentence, each with its own conditions, violation consequences, and authority structures.

Split sentences go by different names across jurisdictions. A judge may impose "180 days followed by two years of probation," or a "suspended sentence with a jail term as a condition of probation," or a "boot camp and probation" structure. In some states, this is called shock probation or shock incarceration, a short, intensive period of confinement designed to precede a longer term of community supervision. The structure varies. The consultant's obligation does not.

What the Consultation Must Cover for Split Sentences

When a client is facing a split sentence, the consultant must explain both pathways in full, not as alternatives, but as sequential realities within the same sentence. That means:

- Explain Pathway One first: the incarceration component, its conditions, the authority structure, and what the client must do during that period to protect the transition to community supervision.
- Explain the transition mechanism: what triggers release from the incarceration component, whether it is automatic or contingent on conduct or program completion, and what the process looks like operationally.
- Explain Pathway Three in full: the probation term that follows, its conditions, the reporting structure, and, critically, that a violation of probation after release can result in return to incarceration on the original sentence.
- Make the connection between the two pathways explicit: conduct during Pathway One affects the conditions of Pathway Three, and a violation of Pathway Three can return the client to Pathway One. The client must understand that the sentence is not finished when they walk out of the facility.

The teach-back at the end of a split sentence consultation must cover both components. Ask the client to explain what happens first, what happens when that ends, and what could send them back. If they cannot restate all three accurately, the consultation is not complete.

Consulting Implication: The Three Pathways Model is a framework for understanding what a sentence is. Split sentences and sequential structures remind us that understanding one pathway is sometimes not enough; the consultant must ensure the client understands the full arc of what the court has ordered, from the first day of confinement to the final day of supervision. Document both pathways in the consultation record, and note explicitly that the transition conditions were explained and confirmed.

Case Study: The Sentence They Thought They Understood

Scenario:

A defendant accepted a plea to community corrections, believing, based on a brief conversation with a family member who had been on probation, that it was essentially the same thing. He understood he would have to 'check in' and 'follow some rules,' but expected to be able to come and go freely and move back home immediately and continue his normal routine. No one had clearly explained that community corrections was a residential placement with curfews, search authority, mandatory programming, and administrative termination.

Consultant's Role:

- Met with the defendant and his attorney prior to plea entry to explain the three pathways in plain terms
- Clearly distinguished community corrections from probation, walking through the facility rules, the daily schedule, and the employment requirement
- Explained administrative termination, including what triggers it and how quickly it can result in a violation of the terms of the plea bargain, resulting in a trip to jail
- Documented the conversation and had the defendant sign an acknowledgment form confirming his understanding

Outcome:

The defendant entered community corrections informed. He was not surprised by the residential requirement, the curfew, or the programming schedule. When a roommate at the facility was terminated for a drug test violation and removed the same day, the defendant understood exactly why and tightened his own compliance as a result. He completed the placement successfully. His attorney later noted that the pre-plea consultation was the single most important step in the entire case.

Conclusion: The Pathway Is the Foundation

Every sentencing consultation is, at its core, an explanation of what a sentence will actually mean in a person's life. That explanation cannot begin in the middle. It must begin at the foundation, with the pathway.

Institutional confinement, structured community placement, and conditional community supervision are not points on a spectrum from harsh to lenient. They are three distinct forms of state authority, each with its own rules, its own risks, and its own relationship between the individual and the system that holds power over them. A consultant who can explain each pathway clearly, in language a client can hold onto and act on, is fulfilling the deepest purpose of this work.

The chapters that follow build on this foundation. Starting with Chapter 4, which addresses the legal duty to inform that makes this explanation not just good practice but a constitutional obligation.

But none of that matters if the pathway itself is not understood first.

Key Takeaways

- Every sentence falls into one of three pathways: Institutional Confinement, Structured Community Placement, or Conditional Community Supervision.
- Institutional confinement removes liberty entirely. County jail and state prison are the same pathway, differentiated only by duration and facility type.
- Structured community placement restores physical liberty but maintains institutional authority, including administrative termination without a court hearing.
- Conditional community supervision (probation) is conditional liberty, not freedom. Violations can result in revocation and incarceration.
- Confusion between pathways is one of the most common sources of uninformed pleas and post-conviction grievances.

- The consultant's first obligation in any consultation is to identify the pathway clearly and ensure the client understands what it means in concrete, practical terms.
- This framework is the foundation on which the legal duty to inform, addressed in Chapter 4, is built.

Chapter 4: The Legal Duty to Inform

Introduction: The Foundation of Fair Decisions

In criminal law, the Sixth Amendment guarantees a defendant's right to effective assistance of counsel. But *effective* means more than simply appearing in court or negotiating a plea. It requires that counsel provide accurate, complete, and comprehensible information so that a client can make an **informed choice**, particularly when deciding whether to accept or reject a plea bargain.

Despite this constitutional safeguard, many defendants still enter pleas without fully understanding the real-world consequences. They may grasp the length of a sentence but not the implications of a sentence to probation versus jail or community corrections versus prison, for example, or the real implications of parole eligibility, collateral impacts, classifications, programming requirements, or facility placement. Others reject favorable pleas based on misinformation or misplaced optimism.

The **duty to inform** is the legal and ethical responsibility that bridges this gap. And it is precisely where the sentencing consultant plays a critical supporting role, helping attorneys ensure that their clients truly comprehend the choices before them.

The Sixth Amendment and the Right to Effective Assistance

The Sixth Amendment provides:

> "In all criminal prosecutions, the accused shall enjoy the right… to have the Assistance of Counsel for his defense."

The Supreme Court has interpreted this right to include not only representation but also **competent advice**, advice that enables a defendant to make reasoned decisions during plea negotiations. When counsel fails to communicate a plea offer, misrepresents its terms, or neglects to explain its consequences, the defendant's constitutional rights are compromised.

The Cornerstone Case: Strickland v. Washington (1984)

In *Strickland v. Washington*, 466 U.S. 668 (1984), the Court articulated the two-pronged test for ineffective assistance of counsel:

1. **Deficient Performance:** Whether counsel's performance fell below an objective standard of reasonableness; and
2. **Prejudice:** The deficient performance affected the outcome of the proceedings. That is, "but for" the deficient performance, the result of the proceedings would have been different.

This framework applies not only to trials and sentencing hearings but also to **plea negotiations**, where over 94 percent of criminal cases are resolved.

Consulting Implication:

Sentencing consultants, while not legal counsel, operate in a space that directly supports the *Strickland* standard. By helping attorneys explain plea terms, sentencing ranges, and consequences in accessible language, consultants enhance the attorney's ability to meet constitutional expectations. Every consultation contributes to preventing future *Strickland*-based claims.

The Communication Mandate: Missouri v. Frye (2012)

In *Missouri v. Frye*, 566 U.S. 134 (2012), the defendant's attorney failed to inform him of a plea offer from the prosecutor before it expired. Frye later pled guilty to more serious charges and received a harsher sentence. The Court held that this failure violated the Sixth Amendment right to effective assistance.

Key Holding:

"[D]efense counsel has the duty to communicate formal offers from the prosecution to accept a plea on terms and conditions that may be favorable to the accused." (at, p. 145).

Consulting Application:

A sentencing consultant can help attorneys fulfill this duty by:

- Reviewing plea paperwork with the client alongside counsel;
- Explaining how the proposed sentence compares to likely trial outcomes;
- Documenting the client's understanding through written acknowledgment forms.

Consultants add an additional layer of clarity and accountability, ensuring that every plea offer is both communicated and comprehended. Their reports can serve as evidence of informed understanding if questions later arise about counsel's performance.

Legal-Ethical Note:

Consultants must never speak with a defendant independently about a plea's legal implications unless the attorney has authorized and is aware of the interaction. Their role is to **support** communication, not replace it.

The Misinformation Problem: Lafler v. Cooper (2012)

In *Lafler v. Cooper*, 566 U.S. 156 (2012), the defendant rejected a plea offer based on his attorney's incorrect advice that the prosecution could not prove intent to murder. After trial, he was convicted and sentenced to a much longer term. The Supreme Court ruled that **erroneous legal advice during plea negotiations** can constitute ineffective assistance under *Strickland.*

Key Holding:

Deficient advice that causes a defendant to reject a plea offer and receive a harsher sentence after trial may establish prejudice under the Sixth Amendment.

Consulting Application:

Sentencing consultants are not legal interpreters, but they are communicative anchors. They help attorneys and clients align expectations with reality. A consultant's function here includes:

- Objectively outlining potential sentence outcomes under both plea and trial scenarios;
- Clarifying how aggravating factors, prior records, or behavior in custody might influence actual time served;
- Reinforcing what counsel has already advised by contextualizing it through the prism of real-world experience.

This process prevents the kind of misunderstanding that led to *Lafler*. Consultants help the client see beyond the abstract; turning for example, an offer of "ten to twenty years" into a tangible, understandable decision.

The Duty to Disclose Collateral Consequences: Padilla v. Kentucky (2010)

While *Frye* and *Lafler* focused on plea negotiations, *Padilla v. Kentucky*, 559 U.S. 356 (2010), expanded the duty to include **collateral consequences**. In *Padilla*, defense counsel failed to advise the defendant, a lawful permanent resident, that pleading guilty to a drug charge would result in deportation. The Court held that this failure violated the Sixth Amendment.

Key Holding:

"When the deportation consequence is clear, counsel must advise the client of this consequence. When it is unclear, counsel must advise that pending criminal charges may carry a risk of adverse immigration consequences."

Consulting Application:

This principle extends beyond immigration. Clients must also be informed of other significant collateral consequences, such as:

- Loss of voting or firearm rights;
- Employment and housing restrictions;
- Ineligibility for certain programs or benefits;
- Parole board considerations and mandatory supervision conditions.

A sentencing consultant assists by identifying these collateral realities and ensuring the client's understanding, especially where systemic consequences extend far beyond the sentence itself.

Practical Integration: The Attorney–Consultant Partnership

An attorney's ethical and constitutional obligations align perfectly with the consultant's purpose. The consultant provides factual and contextual support that strengthens the attorney's representation.

Together, they ensure that:

- Every plea offer is **explained, documented, and comprehended**.
- The client understands both the **legal** and **practical** outcomes.
- The defense team meets the *Frye* and *Lafler* communication standards.
- Collateral consequences, as highlighted in *Padilla*, are meaningfully discussed.

Consultants can also create a record, through signed reports or acknowledgment forms, demonstrating that the client was fully advised and understood the implications of their plea.

Checklist: Attorney–Client Communication Requirements

Before accepting a plea bargain, the attorney and consultant should ensure that the defendant understands:

1. The **charges** and what the plea admits to.
2. The **sentencing range** under the plea versus after trial.
3. **Good time and parole eligibility** implications.
4. **Collateral consequences** (immigration, employment, housing, firearm rights, etc.).
5. **Post-sentence realities** (classification, facility level, programming requirements, and available programs, community supervision).
6. **Appeal rights** that may be waived by the plea.
7. That the **decision is voluntary** and not made under duress or misunderstanding.

This checklist not only protects defendants, but it also protects attorneys from claims of ineffective assistance, legal malpractice, or grievances.

Template: Defendant's Plea Understanding Form

Client Name: ________________________________
Case Number: ________________________________
Date of Consultation: __________________________
Defense Counsel: _____________________________
Sentencing Consultant (if applicable): ______________

I understand that:

1. My attorney has communicated all plea offers made by the prosecution.
2. I have discussed the possible sentence ranges and alternatives to trial.
3. I understand how good time or earned time may affect the length of my incarceration.
4. I understand that parole eligibility does not mean automatic release.
5. I understand that due to the offense I am pleading to, I may be classified by the system accordingly and that I may be required to participate in specific programming.
6. I am aware of the collateral consequences associated with this plea, including potential effects on employment, housing, and civil rights.
7. I have had an opportunity to ask questions and receive clear explanations.
8. I am making this decision voluntarily, with full understanding of its consequences.

Client Signature: ____________________________
Attorney Signature: __________________________
Consultant (Witness) Signature: _________________

(This form should be stored in the attorney's file as documentation of informed consent.)

Documentation as Protection

Detailed documentation not only ensures professionalism but also acts as a safeguard for the defense team. Written summaries, acknowledgment forms, and signed consultation notes can provide clear evidence that a client's decision was informed and voluntary, protecting both the attorney and consultant from future allegations of miscommunication.

In post-conviction proceedings, this type of documentation often becomes the difference between *effective counsel* and *ineffective assistance.* Consultants serve a vital function by helping create that record.

Case Study: Preventing a Lafler Outcome

Scenario:
A defendant is offered a five-year plea for second-degree assault but believes, based on advice from another inmate, that he would "beat it at trial." His attorney brings in a sentencing consultant.

Consultant's Role:

- Reviews the plea with the defendant, explaining realistic trial risks and likely outcomes.
- Breaks down prison classification, parole eligibility, and collateral effects.

- Ensures the client understands that rejecting the plea may result in a sentence exceeding ten years.

The defendant accepts the plea with full comprehension. Later, he expresses relief that he made an informed decision rather than relying on "jailhouse advice." The attorney, supported by the consultant's written documentation, fulfills the *Lafler* duty to inform.

Case Study: The Cost of Not Knowing

Background:

An experienced criminal defense attorney represents a 38-year-old client facing a felony theft charge. The case is not complicated. The evidence is strong, the client has a prior record, and a plea is clearly in his interest. The attorney negotiates a favorable agreement: three years in a state with an earned time credit system, with the realistic possibility of serving closer to twenty months with maximum program participation and clean conduct.

The attorney explains the plea carefully by his own assessment. He tells the client the sentence is three years, that he can get out early for good behavior, and that the facility will be "minimum security, nothing severe." The client nods, signs the acknowledgment form the court requires, and the plea is entered. No sentencing consultant is involved. The attorney considers the matter resolved.

What the attorney did not explain:

- The client's prior record, including a prior institutional violation from a previous sentence in another state, will trigger a medium security classification at intake, not minimum. The conditions at medium security are substantially more restrictive than what the attorney described.

- The earned time credit system in this state requires active program participation, not merely "good behavior." A client who sits idle earns good conduct time only, roughly six days per month, not the full earned time available through programming. The realistic release date without program participation is closer to thirty months, not twenty.

- The plea includes a mandatory condition requiring completion of a cognitive behavioral program that has a six-month waitlist at the facility the client will likely be assigned to. The client's sentence calculation assumes he begins the program immediately. He will not.

- The client has a professional license, a contractor's license, that will be automatically suspended upon felony conviction under state law. He is the sole provider for his family. This consequence is not mentioned at any point before plea entry.

What happens next:

After entering prison, a fellow prisoner informs him that he will have to serve fourteen months before his classification is reviewed and reduced. It won't be until then that he will be eligible to be transferred to a minimum-security facility. The fellow prisoner informs him that he might not even be able to complete the cognitive program because of the wait list for it, and is looking more realistically at serving at least twenty-six months. Six months later than he understood when he entered the plea.

More significantly, he learned that he lost his contractor's license immediately upon conviction. His business collapsed within three months of his entering the system. His family is facing financial crisis.

And he realizes that when he is released, he cannot legally work in his profession at the capacity he once held.

He files a post-conviction motion alleging ineffective assistance of counsel. The motion raises two claims: first, that counsel misrepresented his likely classification and conditions of confinement; second, that counsel failed to advise him of the collateral consequence to his professional license, a consequence that, had he known it, may have led him to seek a different plea structure or go to trial.

The legal exposure:

What Happened	The Legal and Professional Consequence
Misrepresented classification	Client claims he was told "minimum security." He was classified medium. Under Hill v. Lockhart, inaccurate advice about conditions of confinement at the plea stage may support an ineffective assistance claim if the client can show he would not have pleaded guilty had he known the truth.
Earned time miscalculation	The attorney described a release timeline that was not achievable without program participation the client did not know was required. This misrepresentation of how the sentence would actually be served is precisely the type of error the duty to inform is designed to prevent.
Undisclosed collateral consequence	Under Padilla v. Kentucky and its progeny, the duty to inform extends to significant collateral consequences flowing from a conviction. Automatic loss of a professional license, particularly one constituting the client's sole livelihood, is a consequence courts have recognized as sufficiently direct to trigger the disclosure obligation.

No documentation of comprehension	The court-required acknowledgment form was signed, but it contained only general language. There was no consultation summary, no collateral consequence worksheet, no record of what was specifically explained and confirmed. The attorney's file cannot rebut the client's account of what he was told.

What a sentencing consultant would have done:

- Reviewed the client's prior institutional record and flagged that it would affect initial classification, likely medium, not minimum, and explained what medium security conditions actually involve.
- Calculated the earned time timeline accurately, distinguishing between good conduct time (passive) and earned time credits (program-linked), and gave the client a realistic release range under both scenarios.
- Identified the mandatory cognitive program requirement, researched the waitlist at the likely facility, and adjusted the release timeline accordingly, so the client's expectations were grounded in operational reality, not best-case assumptions.
- Flagged the contractor's license consequence to the attorney during case preparation, triggering a conversation about whether the plea could be structured to mitigate or avoid that consequence, a deferred judgment, a reduced charge, or a negotiated condition that preserved the license.
- Completed a collateral consequence worksheet and obtained a signed acknowledgment that the license consequence had been explained and understood.
- Provided the attorney with a written consultation summary documenting everything covered, everything confirmed, and every consequence identified, a record that would have made the post-conviction motion substantially more difficult to sustain.

Note on professional liability: This case study is a composite illustration drawn from common patterns in post-conviction practice.

It is not a description of any specific case. The legal analysis reflects established doctrine under Strickland, Hill, Lafler, and Padilla. Whether any specific set of facts would support a successful ineffective assistance claim depends on the law of the jurisdiction, the facts of the case, and judicial discretion. Sentencing consultants are not attorneys and do not provide legal advice. Their role is to support the attorney's communication function, not to evaluate or predict legal outcomes.

What this case illustrates:

The attorney in this scenario was not incompetent. He was experienced, he negotiated a reasonable plea, and he believed he had explained it adequately. The problem was not negligence in the dramatic sense; it was the gap between what he knew and what the client needed to know, and the absence of any system to identify and close that gap.

That gap is structural. Attorneys are trained to analyze law, evaluate evidence, negotiate outcomes, and advocate before tribunals. They are not trained to translate classification systems, calculate earned time formulas, map collateral consequence landscapes, or verify comprehension through teach-back methodology. No bar admission prepares an attorney to do all of those things in addition to everything else their role requires.

The sentencing consultant exists to do that specific work, not instead of the attorney, but alongside them. When that partnership functions as it should, the client understands what they are agreeing to. The attorney has a documented record of that understanding. And the post-conviction motion described in this case study has no foundation to stand on.

The duty to inform is a constitutional command. The sentencing consultant is one of the most reliable tools available for fulfilling it.

Consulting Implication: Every case involving a plea to incarceration carries some version of the risks described here, misunderstood conditions, miscalculated timelines, undisclosed collateral consequences, and an absence of documentation that could protect the attorney if questions arise later. The consultant's job is not to guarantee outcomes. It is to close the gap between what the attorney explained and what the client genuinely understood, and to leave a written record proving that the gap was closed.

Conclusion: Consultation as a Safeguard of Rights

The duty to inform is not optional, it is a constitutional command. When attorneys and consultants work together, they uphold the principles established by *Strickland*, *Frye*, *Lafler*, and *Padilla*: that justice requires not only fairness in law but understanding in decision-making.

Sentencing consultants serve as the interpreters of consequence, the bridge between legal knowledge and human comprehension. By helping defendants grasp what their choices truly mean, consultants reinforce the integrity of the legal process and the dignity of every person it affects.

Key Takeaways

- The Sixth Amendment guarantees the right to informed, effective legal counsel.
- *Strickland v. Washington* provides the framework; *Frye*, *Lafler*, and *Padilla* apply it to plea practice.
- Sentencing consultants help attorneys meet these duties through clear communication and documentation.
- Proper consultation and recordkeeping protect both client rights and professional reputations.

Chapter 5: Collateral Consequences and Ethical Disclosure

Introduction: The Sentence Beyond the Sentence

When a defendant accepts a plea, they often believe the punishment ends with the number pronounced by the judge. In reality, that number is only the beginning.

Beyond the direct term of imprisonment or probation lies a network of *collateral consequences*, the hidden penalties that follow a conviction into every corner of a person's life. These may include loss of housing opportunities, employment restrictions, parole conditions, registration requirements, and barriers to family reunification.

For many defendants, these unseen consequences have a greater long-term impact than the formal sentence itself. Yet, they are rarely explained in full before a plea is entered.

The consultant's responsibility is to help bridge that gap, translating the law's fine print into real-world understanding. Ethical consultation ensures that defendants grasp not only the punishment imposed by the court but the chain reaction that follows.

Defining Collateral Consequences

Collateral consequences are *non-criminal penalties* triggered automatically by conviction. They are distinct from direct consequences (like incarceration, fines, or probation), which are imposed directly by the court. Collateral consequences are enforced by other laws, agencies, or social systems.

Examples include:

- Loss of voting rights, firearm ownership, or jury eligibility
- Restrictions on housing or public benefits
- Ineligibility for certain jobs, licenses, or educational programs
- Immigration impacts, including deportation or inadmissibility
- Mandatory registration (e.g., sex offender or violent offender registries)
- Parole or community supervision conditions
- Travel and residency restrictions
- Damage to personal relationships, reputation, and ***mental health***

These consequences are extensive, often overlapping, and rarely explained in full at the time of plea. A sentencing consultant can help attorneys anticipate and communicate them, ensuring the client's decision is genuinely informed.

The Legal Foundation: Padilla v. Kentucky (2010)

The landmark case **Padilla v. Kentucky, 559 U.S. 356 (2010)** set the modern standard for disclosing collateral consequences.

Case Summary:

Jose Padilla, a lawful permanent resident of the United States, pled guilty to a drug-distribution charge after his attorney incorrectly told him the conviction would not affect his immigration status. In reality, the plea made him subject to mandatory deportation.

The Supreme Court held that failure to advise a client of clear immigration consequences constituted ineffective assistance of counsel under the Sixth Amendment.

Key Holding:

"When the deportation consequence is truly clear, the duty to give correct advice is equally clear."

Broader Principle:

Although *Padilla* dealt with immigration, its reasoning applies to all major collateral consequences that are *serious, automatic, and foreseeable.* Defendants must be aware of how their conviction will impact their lives beyond incarceration.

Ethical Duty: Informed Consent in Plea Bargaining

Every professional involved in the plea process, attorneys, paralegals, and consultants, shares an ethical duty to promote informed consent.

The **American Bar Association (ABA) Standards for Criminal Justice: Defense Function, §4-5.1** emphasizes that defense counsel should:

"Keep the client informed of developments in the case and the potential consequences of decisions, including collateral consequences."

Consulting Application:

Sentencing consultants reinforce this duty by ensuring the defendant *comprehends* what counsel communicates. Attorneys advise on the law; consultants explain its lived impact. Together, they create a process that satisfies both legal and ethical standards for informed decision-making.

The Expanding Landscape of Collateral Consequences

The collateral effects of conviction have grown dramatically over the past 40 years. The **National Inventory of Collateral Consequences of Conviction (NICCC)** identifies more than **44,000 state and federal laws** that impose restrictions or disabilities on people with criminal records.

These laws affect everything from parenting rights to student loans. Consultants who understand this landscape can help defendants anticipate life after sentencing and can help attorneys reduce risk by ensuring their clients are properly informed.

Common Categories:

1. **Civil and Political Rights**
   - Loss of voting, jury service, or public office eligibility.
   - Restrictions on firearm possession.
2. **Employment and Licensing**

    - Exclusion from certain trades (e.g., law enforcement, healthcare, real estate).
    - Denial of occupational licenses due to felony convictions.
3. **Housing and Public Benefits**
    - Ineligibility for Section 8 or public housing.
    - Denial of TANF, SNAP, or federal student aid (for certain offenses).
    - Background checks for renting houses or apartments.
4. **Family and Custody**
    - Termination or suspension of parental rights in some jurisdictions.
    - Supervised visitation requirements post-release.
5. **Immigration and Travel**
    - Deportation, inadmissibility, or denial of naturalization.
    - Travel restrictions for probationers and parolees.
6. **Community Supervision**
    - Mandatory check-ins, curfews, GPS monitoring, or treatment programs.
    - Residency restrictions and movement limitations.

Consulting Insight Box:

Collateral consequences are often invisible at sentencing but visible for life. The consultant's job is to make the invisible visible before the plea is entered.

Finding the Consequences That Apply: A Practical Guide for Consultants

Knowing that collateral consequences exist is the starting point. Knowing which ones apply to a specific client, in a specific jurisdiction, for a specific offense, is the work. The categories described in the preceding section are universal, but the actual statutes, regulations, and agency policies that impose those consequences vary significantly from state to state and, in some cases, county to county.

Consultants are not expected to memorize every collateral consequence in every jurisdiction. They are expected to know where to look.

The Primary Research Tool

The **Collateral Consequences Resource Center** (CCRC) at *ccresourcecenter.org* maintains the most comprehensive public database of collateral consequences in the United States. The database is organized by state, offense type, and consequence category, and is updated as laws change. It is free to use and does not require registration. Before any consultation involving collateral consequences, search the CCRC database for the client's state and offense. Print or save the relevant results and bring them into the consultation.

A second essential resource is your state's unified judicial or legislative code, which contains the specific statutes imposing licensing restrictions, housing bars, and civil rights limitations. For federal collateral consequences, including immigration bars and federal benefit eligibility, the primary references are the Justice Department's resources and the immigration-specific tools referenced in Chapter 13 of this manual.

What to Do With What You Find

Research produces information. The consultant's job is to translate that information into plain language that the client can absorb and that the attorney can act on. For each applicable consequence identified:

- State the consequence plainly, what it is, when it takes effect, and how long it lasts.
- Identify whether it is automatic upon conviction or triggered by a separate agency action.
- Flag any consequence that requires specialist involvement, immigration, professional licensing, or housing, and ensure the attorney is aware before the consultation closes.
- Document every identified consequence in Form 3 (the Collateral Consequence Review Worksheet) and note whether a referral was made.

Consulting Implication: The research happens before the consultation, not during it. Walk into every session having already identified the applicable consequences for this offense in this jurisdiction. Your preparation is what makes the conversation meaningful and what demonstrates to the attorney that you are a professional resource, not an improvising participant.

Case Integration: Combining Padilla, Frye, and Lafler

The *Padilla* duty to disclose collateral consequences connects directly with *Frye* and *Lafler*'s requirements for effective communication and advice. Together, they form a three-part standard that defines modern ethical practice:

Case	Principle Established	Consulting Implication
Missouri v. Frye (2012)	Counsel must communicate all plea offers	Consultants help clients understand plea terms and sentencing ranges
Lafler v. Cooper (2012)	Incorrect advice causing plea rejection violates Sixth Amendment	Consultants contextualize plea decisions to prevent misinformation

Case	Principle Established	Consulting Implication
Padilla v. Kentucky (2010)	Counsel must disclose clear collateral consequences	Consultants explain real-life impacts of those consequences

When properly integrated, consulting services reinforce all three standards, ensuring that plea decisions meet both **constitutional** and **ethical** thresholds.

Checklist: Collateral Consequences Discussion Guide

Before a client enters a plea, the consultant should work with the defense team to

address the following:

- ✓ Has the attorney explained all direct sentencing outcomes (prison term, probation, fines)?
- ✓ Have collateral consequences, such as loss of housing, job restrictions, or immigration risks, been discussed in detail?
- ✓ Has the consultant helped the client understand how parole, probation, or registry requirements may affect family or employment?
- ✓ Has the client received written material outlining foreseeable consequences?
- ✓ Has the client acknowledged comprehension and voluntariness in writing?
- ✓ Have emotional and mental health considerations been assessed to ensure understanding?

This checklist protects all parties: it safeguards the defendant's rights, documents the attorney's diligence, and demonstrates the consultant's professional value.

Documentation Tools

Collateral Consequence Summary Sheet

Category	Potential Impact	Relevant Agency / Statute	Client Notes
Employment	May lose professional license	Colo. Rev. Stat. §24-5-101	Reviewed 9/12/25
Housing	Not eligible for Section 8 during parole	HUD Policy 982.553	Client acknowledged
Parole	Must reside in approved halfway house	DOC Policy 202.8	Understood by client
Immigration	Mandatory removal (non-citizen)	8 U.S.C. §1227(a)(2)(B)(i)	N/A

Consultants can develop customized charts like this for each client. These records are powerful documentation of due diligence.

Ethics and Professional Boundaries

Sentencing consultants occupy a unique position in the legal ecosystem: they are **educators**, not attorneys. As such, ethical boundaries must be maintained.

Do:

- Clarify that your role is supportive and informational.
- Use accurate, verified legal sources when explaining collateral issues.
- Always coordinate communication through defense counsel.
- Keep detailed records of consultations.

Don't:

- Provide independent legal advice or interpret statutes beyond factual explanation.
- Guarantee or predict judicial outcomes.
- Share client information outside the legal team.

By maintaining these boundaries, consultants protect their credibility and avoid the unauthorized practice of law (UPL).

Case Study: The Hidden Consequences

Scenario:

A young mother accepts a plea for a low-level drug offense. The sentence includes probation and a deferred judgment. Months later, she receives notice that her Section 8 housing assistance is terminated due to the conviction. She and her children lose their home.

Consultant's Role (Hypothetical):

Had a sentencing consultant been involved, they could have identified this risk early by reviewing HUD policies and discussing alternatives with defense counsel. The client might have chosen to fight the charge, seek diversion, or negotiate a non-drug-related plea.

Lesson:

When collateral consequences are left unexplored, clients can face punishments they never anticipated, and attorneys may face grievances, claims of ineffective assistance, or even legal malpractice claims.

Beyond Legal Obligation: The Moral Imperative

The duty to disclose is not merely constitutional, it is moral. The goal of justice is not just procedural fairness, but human understanding. Every defendant deserves to know what they are signing away, what they are walking into, and what they will face upon release.

Consultants bring compassion and clarity to a process that often feels mechanical and impersonal. They remind the system that decisions made in fear or confusion can have lifelong repercussions, and that true justice requires informed consent at every step.

Conclusion: Ensuring the Whole Truth

Collateral consequences form the hidden dimension of every plea bargain. When overlooked, they can devastate lives and undermine faith in the justice system. When acknowledged and explained, they empower defendants to make decisions rooted in understanding.

The consultant's role is to ensure that no one pleads guilty to more than they understand, and that every defendant's "yes" in court is a product of informed, voluntary, and ethically sound consent.

Key Takeaways

- *Padilla v. Kentucky* established the constitutional duty to inform defendants of clear collateral consequences.
- Consultants reinforce this duty by explaining how those consequences play out in real life.
- Ethical consultation requires accuracy, documentation, and respect for role boundaries.
- Transparent communication transforms plea bargaining from a procedural exchange into a process of informed justice.

Chapter 6: The Human Element in Sentencing

Introduction: Justice Is Personal

Every sentencing decision represents a convergence of law, emotion, and identity.
For the attorney, it may be one of dozens of cases on the docket.

For the defendant, it is a single, defining moment that reshapes an entire life.

Fear, shame, anger, and confusion often dominate the decision-making process. Many defendants cannot fully process what they are being told, even when the information is accurate. In these moments, logic alone fails. What's needed is *connection,* the capacity to translate complex legal information into human understanding.

The **sentencing consultant** becomes that translator. They bring empathy, structure, and clarity to conversations charged with emotion. They humanize the process without undermining professionalism, ensuring that clients are not only advised, but *understood.*

The Psychology of Sentencing Decisions

Decision-making under threat activates what psychologists call the **"fight-flight-freeze"** response. When defendants face incarceration, their brains often default to survival mode.

Key effects include:

- **Cognitive overload:** Inability to retain or process detailed information.
- **Distorted risk perception:** Minimizing danger ("I'll beat it at trial") or catastrophizing ("My life is over").
- **Emotional numbness:** Appearing calm while internally dissociating.
- **Reactive behavior:** Making impulsive or self-defeating choices.

Consultants must recognize these reactions not as defiance, but as symptoms of fear and trauma.

When information is delivered with patience and empathy, comprehension improves and anxiety decreases, creating space for informed choice.

Trauma-Informed Consultation

Many justice-involved individuals have long histories of trauma: poverty, violence, abuse, addiction, and institutional betrayal. A trauma-informed consultant understands that emotional safety is a *prerequisite* for learning.

Principles of Trauma-Informed Practice:

1. **Safety:** Create a calm, nonjudgmental environment for discussion.
2. **Trustworthiness:** Be transparent about your role, process, and boundaries.
3. **Choice:** Encourage the client's agency; every question answered reinforces control.
4. **Collaboration:** Work with, not above, the client.

5. **Empowerment:** Highlight strengths, progress, and possibilities for change.

Consulting Insight Box:

"A trauma-informed approach does not excuse behavior, it contextualizes it. Understanding pain allows you to communicate with precision and compassion."

Communicating for Understanding

The goal of consultation is not to display expertise but to ensure comprehension.
Clear communication means meeting clients where they are: linguistically, emotionally, and cognitively.

Practical Communication Strategies:

- **Plain Language:** Replace legal jargon with everyday words.
  - "Deferred judgment" → "The case will be dismissed if you finish probation."
- **Chunking Information:** Deliver details in small, digestible segments.
- **Teach-Back Method:** Ask clients to restate what they understood.
- **Visual Aids:** Use charts, timelines, and sentence-projection tables.
- **Active Listening:** Reflect back emotions ("I hear that you're afraid of losing your kids") before offering information.
- **Cultural Awareness:** Recognize how language, upbringing, and past authority experiences shape trust.

When a consultant uses these strategies, they help transform confusion into comprehension, and fear into focus.

Emotional Intelligence in Practice

Emotional intelligence (EQ) is the ability to recognize, understand, and manage emotions, both your own and others' ("The Six Seconds Model of Emotional Intelligence: EQ in Action").

In sentencing consultation, EQ is as essential as legal knowledge.

Core Competencies:

1. **Self-Awareness:** Knowing your own triggers, biases, and boundaries.
2. **Self-Regulation:** Remaining calm and professional under pressure.
3. **Motivation:** Staying focused on the client's growth, not personal validation.
4. **Empathy:** Seeing the case through the client's emotional lens.
5. **Social Skills:** Communicating clearly, building trust, and defusing conflict.

These competencies build credibility. Attorneys trust consultants who can manage emotionally charged situations; clients trust consultants who can understand them without judgment.

Restoring Humanity to the Process

Sentencing often dehumanizes defendants. Courtrooms speak in terms of "counts," "ranges," and "guidelines," not people.

Consultants help reverse that depersonalization by reframing the defendant as a *person with context* rather than a *case file.*

Ways Consultants Restore Humanity:

- Encourage clients to express fears, hopes, and goals.
- Frame sentencing not as an end, but as a stage in transformation.
- Remind legal teams of the person behind the paperwork.
- Prepare defendants to articulate remorse and accountability authentically in court.

When consultants humanize the process, they contribute not only to better comprehension but also to more meaningful advocacy.

Case Study: The Silent Client

Scenario:

A young defendant accused of robbery refuses to engage during plea discussions. He avoids eye contact, nods mechanically, and answers questions with one-word responses. The attorney fears he doesn't understand the plea but can't get through to him.

Consultant's Approach:

1. Meets privately in a calm setting, away from courtroom noise.
2. Uses open-ended questions: "Tell me what worries you most about this case."
3. Recognizes avoidance as a trauma response, not disrespect.
4. Rephrases the plea terms using visuals, sentence timelines and facility charts.
5. Invites a teach-back: "Can you walk me through what this deal means in your own words?"

Outcome:

The client articulates his understanding and decides to accept the plea. The attorney gains confidence that the plea is voluntary and informed. The consultant's emotional awareness made comprehension possible where formality had failed.

Balancing Empathy and Professionalism

Empathy must never eclipse objectivity. Consultants must remain compassionate without becoming emotionally entangled or advocacy-biased.

Guiding Principles:

- Maintain professional distance: You are a support, not a savior.
- Use empathy to *clarify*, not to *persuade*.
- Document facts objectively, emotion should never distort record-keeping.
- Debrief after emotionally heavy consultations to prevent burnout.

Sustainable compassion comes from boundaries. Without them, empathy can become exhaustion.

When Empathy Meets Resistance: Managing Hostile and Manipulative Clients

Chapter 6 has addressed the client who is silent, frozen by trauma, or overwhelmed by fear. Those situations call for patience, warmth, and careful communication. They are difficult but navigable. There is another category of client behavior that is equally common and requires a different set of tools entirely: the client who is hostile, combative, or attempting to use the consultation for purposes it was not designed to serve.

Hostility and manipulation in the consultation room are not character flaws to be judged. They are frequently responses to a situation the client feels powerless to control. A person facing a decade of incarceration who has never trusted an authority figure, who has been failed by the system before, or who does not understand why yet another professional has been brought into their case, has reasons to be angry and resistant. That context matters, but it does not change the consultant's obligation or their approach.

Common Presentations

Consultants will encounter the following patterns regularly:

- **The disputer**: The client refuses to accept the facts of the charge, insists on relitigating the case, or argues that the evidence is wrong. Every attempt to explain the sentence is interrupted with "but I didn't do it" or "my attorney is useless." The consultation cannot move forward while the client is fighting the premise of the conversation.
- **The deflector:** The client redirects every question toward grievances, about the system, the prosecutor, the attorney, or the judge. They use the consultation as an opportunity to vent, not to learn. Each topic addressed triggers another deflection.
- **The manipulator:** The client attempts to use the consultant against the attorney. "Can you tell my lawyer to reject this plea?" or "My attorney won't listen to me, can you make them?" or, more directly, misrepresenting what the consultant said in front of the attorney to create conflict.
- **The aggressor:** The client becomes verbally hostile, raising their voice, using threatening language, or making the consultation room feel unsafe. This is rare, but it happens, and the consultant must know how to respond.

How to Respond

The approach differs by presentation, but the underlying principle is the same: you are not in the room to be right, to win, or to force acceptance. You are in the room to ensure comprehension. Everything you do serves that purpose, including stopping when that purpose cannot be served.

For the disputer: Acknowledge the feeling without entering the argument. "I hear that you believe the charges are wrong, and that is something for you and your attorney to work through. My job today is to make sure you understand what this plea would mean if you accepted it — not to tell you whether to accept it. Can we start there?" Redirect once, clearly. If the disputation continues and genuine comprehension is not possible, pause the session.

For the deflector: Name what is happening without judgment. "I can tell there's a lot you want to get off your chest, and that makes sense given what you're going through. But I have a limited amount of time with you today, and I want to use it in a way that actually helps you. Can I ask you to hold those concerns until we've covered the basics, and then we can come back to them?" Set a structure. Most deflectors will follow it.

For the manipulator: Be clear and direct about your role the moment a boundary is tested. "My job is not to advise your attorney or to relay messages between you. My job is to help you understand what your attorney has already negotiated. If you have concerns about the legal strategy, that conversation belongs with your attorney directly — and I'd encourage you to have it." Document any attempt to use the consultation to undermine or circumvent the attorney, and notify the attorney in writing.

For the aggressor: Do not match the energy. Keep your voice calm and your posture neutral. "I understand you're frustrated, and I'm not going to take that personally. But I need the conversation to stay at a level where we can both do our jobs. If we can't get there today, I'm going to let your attorney know and we'll find a better time." If the client becomes physically threatening, end the session immediately and ensure the attorney is notified.

Case Study: The Client Who Wanted to Fight

Scenario:

A 29-year-old client is referred for consultation before accepting a plea to aggravated assault. He enters the session angry, insisting the charges are exaggerated and that his attorney "sold him out" by recommending the plea. Before the consultant can begin, he demands to know why another stranger is involved in his case and whether the consultant is "on the government's side."

Consultant's Approach:

- Acknowledges the frustration directly and without defensiveness: "That's a fair question. I'm not connected to the prosecution or the court. I was brought in by your attorney because my job is to explain what this sentence actually means in practice, not to tell you what to do."
- Does not attempt to defend the attorney or the plea. Stays focused on purpose: "I'm not here to convince you of anything. I'm here to make sure that whatever you decide, you decide it knowing exactly what you're agreeing to."
- Offers the client a concrete task: "I'm going to ask you to listen for about twenty minutes. After that, if you have questions or you want to push back on anything I've said, I want to hear it. Can we try that?"
- The client agrees. The session proceeds. At the end, he restates the pathway, the release mechanism, and the collateral

consequences accurately, and acknowledges, unprompted, that there was information he did not have before.

What This Illustrates:

Hostility at the start of a consultation does not mean the session will fail. It often means the client has not had anyone take their frustration seriously before asking them to engage. The consultant who holds their ground calmly, names the purpose of the session clearly, and offers the client a structured way to participate, rather than demanding compliance, frequently finds that the resistance dissolves once the client feels heard.

What it never means: continuing a session that has become unsafe, or allowing the consultation room to become a venue for relitigating the case, attacking the attorney, or generating documentation under conditions that do not reflect genuine comprehension.

Consulting Implication: Document the presenting behavior, your response, and the outcome. If the session was productive despite a difficult opening, that is worth recording; it demonstrates that the client's comprehension was achieved under real conditions, not ideal ones. If the session had to be paused or terminated, document that too, along with the reason and the communication made to the attorney. Your record should reflect what actually happened in the room.

When the Human Element Exceeds Your Scope: Recognizing the Limits of Consultation

Emotional intelligence and trauma-informed communication make you a more effective consultant. They do not make you a clinician. There is a line, sometimes clear, sometimes blurry, between a client who is emotionally distressed and a client who is experiencing a mental health crisis that requires professional intervention. Knowing where that line is, and what to do when a client approaches or crosses it, is one of the most important professional judgments a consultant makes.

The sentencing consultation room is not a therapy session. You are not equipped, and not authorized, to diagnose, treat, or manage acute mental health conditions, suicidal ideation, psychotic episodes, or severe trauma responses. Proceeding with a consultation when a client is in crisis does not help the client. It produces a document that does not reflect genuine comprehension and may later be challenged as a basis for informed consent.

Signs That a Consultation Should Stop

The following are indicators that the session should be paused and the attorney notified before proceeding:

- The client is unable to track the conversation or maintain basic comprehension across multiple careful attempts at explanation.
- The client appears to be dissociating, responding with flat affect, absent gaze, or answers that do not correspond to the questions asked.
- The client discloses active suicidal ideation or intent to harm themselves or others.
- The client is visibly intoxicated, in acute withdrawal, or otherwise chemically impaired in a way that prevents meaningful participation.
- The client becomes so distressed, unable to speak, shaking, unreachable, that proceeding would require them to make decisions under conditions of acute emotional dysregulation.

None of these situations is a reason to abandon the client. They are reasons to stop the consultation, contact the attorney, and ensure that the appropriate support, a mental health professional, a forensic psychologist, or at minimum, a rescheduled session after the client has stabilized, is in place before proceeding.

When a Client Expresses Active Suicidal Intent: An Immediate Response Protocol

The general guidance to pause a session and notify the attorney applies to most crisis presentations. One situation demands a more specific and more urgent response: when a client expresses active suicidal ideation, stating directly or strongly implying that they intend to end their life.

This is not a situation that can be managed with a rescheduled session. It is a safety emergency. The consultant's obligation in this moment is clear, sequential, and non-negotiable. It does not require clinical training to fulfill. It requires following a defined protocol without deviation.

IMPORTANT—IMMEDIATE ACTION REQUIRED: If a client expresses active suicidal intent during a consultation, in a jail, detention facility, attorney's office, or any other setting, stop the consultation immediately and follow the protocol below. Do not attempt to assess the severity yourself. Do not attempt clinical intervention. Do not leave the client unattended.

The Five-Step Protocol

Step 1: Stop the consultation immediately. Do not attempt to continue, redirect, or complete any portion of the session. Put down your forms. The consultation is over for today.

Step 2: Acknowledge the client directly and calmly. Do not show alarm, argue, or minimize. Say: "I hear you. I'm taking that seriously. I'm going to make sure you have the right support right now." Then stay present and keep the client calm while the next steps are taken.

Step 3: Notify facility staff or security immediately if the consultation is taking place in a jail, detention center, or correctional facility. Tell them directly: "I need staff assistance. My client has expressed suicidal intent." Do not attempt to manage the situation alone. If the consultation is taking place in an attorney's office or other non-institutional setting, call 911.

Step 4: Notify the attorney. Contact defense counsel by phone as soon as facility staff or emergency services have been engaged. Do not wait until after the fact. The attorney must be informed in real time, not through a follow-up email.

Step 5: Document everything in writing as soon as the immediate situation is resolved. Record the exact words the client used, the time, the setting, the actions you took, who you notified, and when. This documentation protects the client, the attorney, and the integrity of the consultation record. It is not optional and it should not be summarized, write down what the client actually said.

What Not to Do

- Do not attempt to assess whether the client is "serious." You are not qualified to make that determination, and the consequences of being wrong are irreversible.
- Do not ask probing clinical questions about the client's history, means, or plan. That is a clinical assessment function that belongs to a mental health professional.
- Do not leave the client alone while you make notifications. If you must step away to contact staff, ensure that another person, facility staff, the attorney, or another responsible adult is with the client before you leave the room.
- Do not complete or finalize any consultation documentation from that session as if the session were productive. A consultation that ended due to a safety crisis does not generate a comprehension acknowledgment.
- Do not attempt to reschedule the consultation in the same communication in which you are addressing the safety crisis.

> That conversation happens later, through the attorney, once the client has received appropriate support.

After the Immediate Crisis

Once the client has been transferred to appropriate care, the consultant's follow-up obligations run through the attorney, not directly to the client. Notify the attorney in writing of what occurred, what actions were taken, and what documentation exists. The attorney decides whether and when to reschedule the consultation, what mental health assessment or support should be in place first, and whether any special accommodations are needed for the next session.

Do not contact the client directly after a safety crisis without explicit authorization from defense counsel. The attorney-client relationship governs what communication is appropriate, and the attorney needs to manage that relationship in the aftermath of a crisis without third-party contact complicating it.

Consulting Implication: Following this protocol is not about liability protection, though it does protect everyone involved. It is about the fundamental obligation you accepted when you entered this work: the person across from you is a human being in the most consequential and often most desperate period of their life. When they reach the point of expressing that they do not want to continue living, the consultation is no longer the priority. They are. The protocol exists to make sure you know exactly what to do in that moment, so that you can do it without hesitation.

What to Say and What to Do

When a consultation must stop for these reasons, the approach is straightforward. Tell the client:

"I want to make sure we do this right, and I don't think today is the right day to do it. I'm going to let your attorney know so we can find a better time. That's not a problem, it's just the right call."

Document what you observed, not a clinical assessment, but a factual description of behavior, and communicate it to the attorney in writing. Note the date, what you observed, and that you paused the session. Note any referral the attorney subsequently makes. This documentation protects the client, the attorney, and the consultation record.

Chapter 13 of this manual addresses special populations in detail, including clients with mental health diagnoses and the referral resources appropriate for each. Any client presentation that raises clinical concerns should be approached using that chapter's framework.

Consulting Implication: Stopping a consultation when a client is in crisis is not a failure. It is the correct professional judgment. A consultation that produces a signed form without genuine comprehension is not informed consent; it is paperwork. The attorney and the client are both better served by a session that happens when the client can actually participate in it.

Cultural and Generational Awareness

Sentencing does not occur in a vacuum. Culture, age, and community norms shape how individuals perceive authority, guilt, and justice.

Examples:

- Clients from collectivist backgrounds may prioritize family reputation over personal freedom.
- Younger defendants may struggle with abstract time concepts ("five years" feels infinite).

- Communities with historical mistrust of legal institutions may interpret professional distance as disrespect.

Consultants who understand these dynamics can tailor their communication accordingly, respecting cultural identity while maintaining legal accuracy.

Checklist: The Human-Centered Consultation

✓ Establish psychological safety before discussing legal matters.
✓ Explain complex terms in plain language.
✓ Allow time for emotional processing and questions.
✓ Use visuals or analogies suited to the client's learning style.
✓ Employ the teach-back method to confirm understanding.
✓ Maintain professionalism and clear boundaries at all times.
✓ End every session with empowerment, emphasize agency, and next steps.

Ethical Reflection: Dignity as a Legal Value

Ethics in sentencing consultation extends beyond confidentiality or competence. It includes the moral responsibility to preserve dignity. Every interaction with a client, tone, posture, and language communicates whether they are seen as a person or a problem.

When consultants treat clients with dignity, they affirm the justice system's higher purpose: not merely to punish wrongdoing, but to affirm human worth even in accountability.

Conclusion: The Heart of Effective Consultation

The human element is not a soft skill; it is a professional standard.

Empathy without structure leads to confusion; structure without empathy leads to detachment. True effectiveness lies in the synthesis of both.

By practicing trauma-informed communication, emotional intelligence, and cultural humility, sentencing consultants transform fear into understanding and shame into agency. They remind attorneys, courts, and clients alike that justice is not only about the law, but also about people.

Key Takeaways

- Emotional intelligence and trauma awareness are essential to effective consultation.
- Clear, plain-language communication ensures comprehension and trust.
- Consultants humanize sentencing by restoring dignity to clients often dehumanized by the process.
- Empathy must be balanced with professionalism and boundaries to remain ethical and sustainable.

Chapter 7: Conducting Effective Consultations

Introduction: Turning Insight into Structure

By this stage, the consultant's purpose is clear: to bridge the gap between the legal process and human understanding. But to perform that role effectively, a consultant must move beyond good intentions and empathy into **procedure**; a consistent, structured approach that ensures accuracy, professionalism, and ethical compliance.

Every consultation, no matter the case type or sentence length, should follow a deliberate process that combines preparation, communication, documentation, and reflection. Structure builds credibility; it signals to attorneys that your service is not improvisational but professional.

This chapter outlines a complete step-by-step framework for conducting effective sentencing consultations, from initial referral to written summary. It includes templates, ethical boundaries, and communication checkpoints that align with both **Sixth Amendment standards** and **professional best practices.**

The Five Phases of Consultation

The sentencing consultation process can be organized into five distinct phases:

1. **Preparation:** Gathering facts, reviewing case documents, and coordinating with counsel.

2. **Intake:** Building rapport, clarifying roles, and setting expectations with the client.
3. **Consultation:** Delivering information, clarifying understanding, and addressing questions.
4. **Documentation:** Recording the discussion, confirming comprehension, and safeguarding confidentiality.
5. **Follow-Up:** Providing written summaries, referrals, or additional clarification as needed.

Each phase contributes to a transparent, legally sound, and ethically defensible consultation.

Phase 1: Preparation

A. Gather Case Information

Before meeting a client, the consultant should review key materials provided by defense counsel:

- Charging documents and discovery summary
- Plea offer(s) and sentencing range
- Criminal history and pre-sentence reports (PSI, if available)
- Notes on client background or mental health concerns
- Any mitigation materials (letters, education or treatment certificates, etc.)

Consulting Tip:

Never review or discuss materials that have not been cleared by defense counsel. ***Maintain the sanctity of attorney-client privilege at all times.***

B. Understand Attorney Objectives

Communicate directly with the attorney to clarify:

- What questions or concerns the client has expressed
- The attorney's legal strategy and desired outcomes
- Whether the consultation should focus on understanding, decision support, or post-sentencing preparation

This step ensures alignment; the consultant supports, but never substitutes for, the attorney's role.

Phase 2: Intake and Establishing Trust

A. Setting the Tone

The initial interaction determines the effectiveness of the entire session. Begin with transparency:

- Explain your background and role clearly ("I'm here to help you understand the options your attorney has explained.")
- Emphasize confidentiality and professionalism.
- Clarify that you are not a lawyer, that you do not give legal advice or make promises about outcomes.

Ethical Introduction Script:

"I'm not your attorney, I am not an attorney, and I don't make any decisions in your case. My job is to make sure you understand everything that's being discussed: the plea offer, the sentence, and what life will look like afterward."

B. Rapport-Building Techniques

- Use open body language and attentive listening.
- Begin with neutral, simple questions: "How are you holding up?" or "What's been hardest to understand so far?"
- Recognize that many clients are intimidated by legal professionals; your tone should be calm, clear, and human.

C. Identify the Client's Knowledge Baseline

Ask what the client already understands about their charges and plea. This avoids redundancy and reveals misconceptions early.

Example:

- "Tell me what you believe your sentence would be if you took this deal."
- "What do you think happens if you go to trial instead?"

These questions set the stage for corrective education.

Phase 3: The Consultation Session

A. Explain, Don't Overwhelm

Information overload can cause confusion and anxiety. Focus on clarity:

- Present information in layers; start with the big picture, then move to details.
- Translate legal terms into plain English.
- Use visual aids (charts, timelines, or program flow diagrams).

Example Breakdown:

Legal Term	Plain Explanation
"Deferred sentence"	You'll be on probation, and if you complete it successfully, the conviction can be dismissed.
"Concurrent sentence"	You serve multiple sentences at the same time.
"Consecutive sentence"	You serve multiple sentences as one big sentence.
"Parole eligible in five years"	After serving five years, you can apply for release based on good behavior.

B. Clarify Plea and Sentencing Scenarios

Discuss both possible paths:

1. **If the client accepts the plea:** explain projected sentence, facility type, parole eligibility, potential program requirements, and collateral consequences.
2. **If the client goes to trial:** outline potential exposure, trial risks, and sentencing ranges.

Consultants should present factual comparisons without advocacy bias; the attorney leads strategy, the consultant clarifies consequences.

C. Address Emotional Barriers

Use trauma-informed communication principles:

- Pause often to allow emotional processing.
- Validate fear and confusion ("It makes sense you'd feel that way.").

- Use teach-back: "Can you explain in your own words what you understand this plea means?"

D. Encourage Questions

Clients often hesitate to ask questions for fear of appearing ignorant. Reassure them:

> "There are no bad questions in this room. The more you ask, the better decisions you can make."

Encourage written notes or provide a handout summarizing key points.

Phase 4: Documentation and Recordkeeping

Documentation serves both practical and legal purposes. It provides a record of understanding and protects all parties from future disputes.

A. Consultation Summary Report (Template)

Client Name: ______________________________
Case Number: ______________________________
Date: ______________________
Defense Counsel: ______________________
Consultant: ___________________________

Purpose of Consultation:
(e.g., Plea offer clarification, sentencing expectations, collateral consequences)

Topics Covered:

- Sentencing range and parole eligibility

- Facility classification and incarceration conditions
- Collateral consequences (employment, housing, family)
- Emotional/psychological concerns identified

Client Understanding (Teach-Back Summary):
(Record client's explanation in their own words of what they understood.)

Follow-Up Recommendations:

- Review with counsel prior to final plea
- Provide written collateral consequence sheet
- Schedule post-sentencing consultation (if needed)

Signatures:

- Client: ______________________________
- Attorney: _____________________________
- Consultant: ___________________________

This form creates a record of due diligence and can be stored securely in the attorney's client file.

B. Confidentiality Protocols

- Store all documents securely (encrypted or locked file).
- Never share reports with external parties without written authorization from defense counsel.
- Delete digital copies upon case closure, per agreement.
- Include confidentiality disclaimers in written materials.

C. Ethical Disclaimer Example

"This consultation was conducted for educational and informational purposes to assist defense counsel in ensuring client comprehension.

The consultant does not provide legal advice or make representations regarding case outcomes."

Phase 5: Follow-Up and Ongoing Support

A. Provide a Written Summary

Within 24 to 48 hours, deliver a concise summary to defense counsel, including:

- Key topics covered
- Client's level of understanding
- Any concerns requiring clarification
- Recommended next steps

B. Post-Sentencing Consultation (Optional)

Some clients benefit from a follow-up session after sentencing to discuss:

- Facility placement expectations
- Parole and good time policies
- Reentry planning and community resources

These services strengthen long-term client outcomes and reinforce your reputation for holistic, professional care.

"The Five Phases of Consultation"

The Five Phases established the when and the how of a consultation: preparation, intake, session, documentation, and follow-up. The Consultation Sequence addresses the what: the specific content that must be covered during Phase 3, the session itself, in a consistent order that applies to every client and every pathway.

The sequence has six steps. Each step builds on the one before it. Together they form a complete system for fulfilling the duty to inform, one that a consultant can learn, practice, and deliver reliably across every case they handle.

> *The Consultation Sequence operates within Phase 3 of the Five Phases framework. It does not replace preparation (Phase 1), intake (Phase 2), documentation (Phase 4), or follow-up (Phase 5). It provides the content architecture for the session itself.*

#	Step	What to Cover	Verify Before Moving On
1	**Identify the Pathway** *The Three Pathways Model*	• Name the pathway: Institutional Confinement, Structured Community Placement, or Conditional Community Supervision. • Explain what that pathway means in plain terms, not a legal category, but a lived reality. • Name the most common misconception for this pathway and correct it explicitly. • Ask: "In your own words, what kind of sentence is this?"	☐ Client can name the pathway. ☐ Client can state what it means for their daily life. ☐ Misconception corrected and confirmed.
2	**Map the Authority Structure**	• Identify who holds authority over the client during this sentence: institution, facility staff,	☐ Client understands who controls their daily life.

	Who controls what, and what that means	probation officer, parole board. • Explain what that authority can do: restrict movement, impose discipline, terminate placement, revoke supervision. • For Pathway Two: explain administrative termination, staff can return to incarceration without a hearing. • For Pathway Three: explain revocation, court can impose suspended sentence upon violation.	☐ Client understands what violation consequences look like in this pathway.
3	**Explain Daily Reality** *What the sentence actually feels like*	• Describe the intake process: how long, what assessments occur, contact restrictions during that period. • Explain classification: what level is likely, what determines it, and what it means for conditions and programming. • For incarceration: describe facility type, daily schedule, visitation, programming access. • For community placement: describe facility rules, curfew, employment requirements, search authority.	☐ Client can describe what their first weeks will look like. ☐ Family has been told about contact restrictions. ☐ Client understands classification.

		• For supervision: describe reporting, conditions, and what triggers a violation report.	
	Explain Failure Consequenc es *What a violation costs in concrete terms*	• Name the consequence of a serious disciplinary violation in this system: days forfeited, reclassification, segregation. • Calculate it: "In this state, a Class I violation costs 90 days of earned time credits." • For indeterminate states: explain how violations affect the parole board's assessment. • For community placement: explain that administrative termination returns them to incarceration without a hearing. • Make the cost real, not abstract: connect it to time, to family contact, to the release date.	☐ Client can state what a serious violation costs in concrete terms. ☐ Client understands this is not hypothetical, it happens regularly.
5	**Explain the Release Mechanism** *When do I actually come home?*	• Identify the applicable system: indeterminate parole, determinate formula, or federal good conduct time / FSA credits. • Calculate the realistic release range: best case	☐ Client can state which release mechanism governs their sentence.

		(maximum credits, clean record), likely case, and worst case. • For indeterminate: explain what the parole board looks for, record, programming, release plan. • For determinate: show the math. Sentence minus good time minus earned time = projected release. • For federal: explain the 85-percent floor, good conduct time cap, and First Step Act credits. • Address post-release supervision: it is part of the sentence, not the end of it.	☐ Client can give a realistic release range. ☐ Client understands post-release supervision applies.
6	**Confirm Comprehension** *Teach-back, the non-negotiable final step*	• Do not ask yes/no questions. Ask the client to explain in their own words. • "Tell me what kind of sentence this is and what it means for your daily life." • "When do you expect to come home, and what determines that?" • "What happens if you get a serious write-up in the first year?" • If the client cannot restate accurately: return to the relevant step. Do not sign forms until	☐ Client restated pathway correctly. ☐ Client restated release mechanism correctly. ☐ Client restated violation consequence correctly. ☐ Forms signed only after all three confirmed.

	comprehension is confirmed. • Document the teach-back responses verbatim in the consultation record.	

The six steps work as a system, not a checklist. Moving through them in order ensures that each piece of information lands on the foundation of the piece before it. A client who understands the pathway before hearing about the release mechanism is a different client from one who hears those things in reverse order, or not at all.

Step 6, Confirm Comprehension, is the only step that cannot be shortened or skipped under any circumstance. Every other step is about delivering information. Step 6 is about verifying that information was received. The consultation is not complete until the client can restate, in their own words, the pathway, the release mechanism, and the cost of a serious violation. If they cannot, return to the relevant step. Do not collect signatures. Do not close the session.

Consulting Implication: Use this sequence as your in-room guide. Keep it visible during the session. After each step, check the verification column before moving forward. At the end of every session, your consultation record should show what the client said at Step 6, verbatim, in their own words. That record is the evidence that the duty to inform was actually fulfilled.

Best Practices for Effective Consulting

1. **Always Work Through Counsel:**
   Never consult independently with a represented client.
2. **Stay Within Role:**
   Provide information, not legal interpretation.

3. **Use Plain Language:**
   Replace jargon with accessible explanations.
4. **Document Everything:**
   Every session should result in a record that can withstand legal scrutiny.
5. **Reflect and Adjust:**
   After each consultation, note what worked, what confused the client, and how your process could improve.
6. **Continuous Learning:**
   Keep updated on sentencing reforms, correctional policy, and relevant case law.

Consulting Insight Box:

Informed clients make fewer mistakes, fewer complaints, and more meaningful commitments to change. The consultant's structure is the system's safety net.

Case Study: Structured Consultation Prevents Misunderstanding

Scenario:

An attorney refers a client for consultation before accepting a complex plea involving concurrent and consecutive sentences. The client insists he "only has to do eight years," though the paperwork indicates otherwise.

Consultant's Actions:

- Reviews case documents with counsel.
- Explains the difference between concurrent and consecutive sentences using a visual timeline.
- Confirms understanding through teach-back: "So, tell me when you think you'll be eligible for release."

- The client initially says "eight," then pauses and self-corrects after clarification: "No, it's actually fourteen before parole."

Outcome:

The attorney finalizes the plea with full confidence that the client understands the real exposure. The signed report and summary form protect all parties from future misunderstanding or appeal claims.

Tools for Professional Efficiency

- **Client Intake Form:** gathers demographic and case details.
- **Consultation Report Template:** formalizes the structure of every session.
- **Confidentiality Agreement:** defines limits of disclosure and data handling.
- **Plea Understanding Form:** verifies comprehension.
- **Collateral Consequence Summary Sheet:** accompanies each consultation.
- **Session Debrief Log:** consultant's private reflections for continuous improvement.

These tools form the foundation of a repeatable system, one that builds both legal credibility and professional trust.

Conclusion: Structure Builds Legitimacy

Effective consultation is equal parts empathy and procedure. Without structure, good intentions become disorganization. Without empathy, structure becomes mechanical.

A disciplined consultation process assures attorneys that you operate with the same professionalism they do: accountable, consistent, and ethical. It assures clients that their understanding matters, that they are not just a case file, and that the system can still speak in human terms.

Through this process, the sentencing consultant becomes an indispensable part of the defense team, not as a legal actor, but as a bridge between law and life.

Key Takeaways

- Structure is the backbone of credibility.
- Follow the five phases: Preparation, Intake, Consultation, Documentation, and Follow-Up.
- Document everything; clarity protects everyone.
- Work through counsel, stay in role, and maintain strict confidentiality.
- A professional system transforms compassion into measurable impact.

Chapter 8: Working Effectively with Attorneys

Introduction: Partnership, Not Performance

The sentencing consultant's effectiveness depends on one core principle: **collaboration, not competition**.

Attorneys lead the defense strategy; consultants strengthen its foundation. The relationship works best when both roles are clearly understood and mutually respected.

Attorneys manage the *law*; motions, negotiations, and constitutional protections. Consultants manage the *lived realities*; helping ensure that the defendant truly understands the plea, the sentence, and what follows.

When done well, this partnership not only protects the client's rights but also enhances the attorney's performance under the **Sixth Amendment's duty of effective assistance**. A strong attorney-consultant relationship reduces client confusion, eliminates miscommunication, and prevents post-conviction claims rooted in misunderstanding.

Understanding the Attorney's Perspective

Before you can support an attorney, you must understand the pressures they face. Most criminal defense lawyers balance **high caseloads**, **limited time**, **limited resources**, and **emotional exhaustion**. Their professional identity revolves around advocacy, procedure, and precision, not always patient explanation.

Many clients misunderstand plea terms or sentencing realities, and attorneys often don't have the bandwidth to bridge that gap thoroughly.

That's where your value lies.

When you approach attorneys with empathy for their workload and respect for their role, you'll position yourself as a partner who lightens their burden, not someone competing for authority.

Consulting Insight Box:

Defense attorneys already fight the battle in court. The consultant's job is to win the battle of understanding before the client ever steps in front of a judge.

Clarifying Roles and Boundaries

The Attorney's Role

- Provides legal advice and representation.
- Negotiates plea offers, argues motions, and manages case strategy.
- Bears the ultimate responsibility for ethical and constitutional compliance.

The Consultant's Role

- Educates clients about sentencing realities, prison conditions, and collateral consequences.

Inside the Sentence

- Enhances attorney-client communication by translating legal concepts into plain language.
- Documents client comprehension through reports and acknowledgment forms.
- Offers insight into institutional processes (classification, parole, reentry) that affect sentencing outcomes.

The Line Not to Cross

Consultants must **never**:

- Offer legal advice or opinions on case strategy.
- Negotiate directly with prosecutors or court staff.
- Make promises about outcomes.
- Undermine counsel's authority.

Your credibility depends on respecting these boundaries without exception. When in doubt, always defer to the attorney.

Building Trust and Professional Rapport

1. Professionalism from the First Contact

When introducing yourself to an attorney, lead with your **credentials, your purpose, and the clarity of your role**.

Attorneys value organization and concise communication.

Sample Introduction (Email):

Subject: Sentencing Consultation Support for [Client Name, Case #]

Dear [Attorney Name],

My name is [Your Name], and I work as a sentencing consultant specializing in plea comprehension and collateral consequence analysis. My role is to assist defense counsel by helping clients fully understand their plea offers, sentencing exposure, and post-conviction realities.

I understand your time is valuable. My process is designed to support your representation, not to interpret the law, by documenting client comprehension and addressing practical concerns that may arise before sentencing.

I look forward to working under your direction to ensure the best outcomes for your client.

Respectfully,
[Your Name, Credentials]
[Contact Information]

This tone projects professionalism, clarity, and respect for the attorney's authority, the foundation of trust.

2. Understanding Communication Preferences

Each attorney has their own workflow. Some prefer detailed written reports; others want short debriefs by phone. Always ask:

"How would you like updates after client sessions? A written report, a summary email, or verbal feedback?"

Adapting to their style shows flexibility and reinforces your value as a collaborative partner.

3. Confidentiality and Attorney-Client Privilege

When you're engaged by defense counsel, your work falls under the **umbrella of attorney-client privilege**, but only if structured properly.

Best Practices:

- Always receive written confirmation that you are working under the attorney's direction.
- Keep all communications confidential and routed through counsel.
- Never share client information outside the defense team.
- Mark all reports as *"Confidential – Prepared at the Direction of Defense Counsel."*

Sample Disclaimer:

"This report was prepared at the request and direction of defense counsel for the purpose of facilitating attorney-client communication and is protected by privilege. It should not be distributed beyond the defense team without counsel's authorization."

This approach safeguards the attorney, the client, and your own professional liability.

Integrating the Consultant's Work into the Legal Process

Attorneys will be most receptive to your input when your findings directly support their strategy and documentation.

A. Consultation Summaries

Provide concise, factual summaries that capture what the client understood, not opinions or interpretations.

Example (Excerpt):

The client demonstrated clear understanding of the sentencing range and parole eligibility dates. When asked to explain in his own words, he correctly identified the difference between the plea term and trial exposure. He acknowledged awareness of the potential impact on employment and housing.

Avoid editorializing or moral commentary. Keep tone neutral and professional.

B. Written Reports as Exhibits

In some cases, attorneys may request a consultant's written report for inclusion in mitigation packets or plea documentation.

Ensure your writing:

- Is objective and fact-based;
- Avoids advocacy language ("the client deserves leniency");
- Uses neutral phrasing ("The client has completed consultation and demonstrated understanding of sentencing implications.").

These documents enhance the record of informed consent, reducing appellate risk for the attorney.

The Consultant's Communication Toolkit

To collaborate effectively with attorneys, maintain a professional toolkit of standardized documents:

Tool	Purpose
Referral Agreement	Defines scope, privilege, and confidentiality.
Consultation Summary Form	Provides structure for written feedback.
Email Template Library	Ensures consistent, concise communication.
Plea Understanding Form	Documents client comprehension.
Confidentiality Statement	Protects privilege and ethical boundaries.
Professional Resume and CV	Establishes your expertise when working with new firms.

By providing structured, clean materials, you signal reliability and professionalism, qualities attorneys value above all else.

Collaborating on Complex Cases

In multi-defendant or high-profile cases, consultants may interact with multiple attorneys or mitigation specialists.

Maintain clarity by:

- Confirming which attorney you report to.
- Using consistent language across teams.
- Keeping each report distinct and confidential.

- Avoiding casual conversation about case details outside scheduled discussions.

Professional restraint earns trust, and often, repeat referrals.

Addressing Common Challenges

1. The Overprotective Attorney

Some attorneys may initially see you as unnecessary or intrusive. Avoid defensiveness. Instead, demonstrate how your consultation complements their work.

"I see my role as supporting your client's understanding so you can focus on strategy. I never discuss legal advice, only comprehension and consequences."

2. The Skeptical Client

Clients may mistrust new faces. Reassure them that you work under the attorney's direction and that everything remains confidential.

"Your attorney asked me to help make sure everything about your plea and sentence makes sense to you. My role is to help you understand, not to judge."

3. Role Creep

Sometimes, attorneys or clients may ask you to do more than your scope allows. Maintain your boundaries respectfully:

"That's a legal question best addressed by your attorney. I can explain how it might play out in practice, but I'll defer to counsel on the law."

Boundaries protect your professional credibility.

Case Study: The Partnership That Prevented a Post-Conviction Claim

Scenario:

A public defender's office faced a recurring problem: clients filing post-conviction claims alleging they didn't understand plea agreements. The supervising attorney decided to integrate sentencing consultation as part of the pre-plea process.

Outcome:

- Consultants conducted standardized sessions before every plea.
- Clients signed comprehension acknowledgment forms.
- Attorneys noted improved client cooperation and fewer disciplinary grievances.
- Within one year, the office saw a measurable decline in Rule 35(c) ineffective-assistance filings.

The partnership demonstrated that structured consultation not only enhanced client understanding but also strengthened legal defense integrity.

Maintaining Professional Reputation

Attorneys are your most powerful source of credibility and referral. To maintain and expand that trust:

- Deliver on time.
- Communicate concisely.
- Keep documentation clean, confidential, and organized.
- Never gossip or speculate about cases or clients.
- Seek continuing education in criminal law and ethics.

Professionalism is your brand. When attorneys see that your methods consistently make their jobs easier and their clients better informed, your value becomes self-evident.

Sample Referral Agreement

Sentencing Consultation Referral Agreement

This agreement confirms that **[Consultant Name]** will provide sentencing consultation services for **[Client Name]** at the request and direction of **[Attorney Name / Firm]**.

Scope of Work: Consultation limited to clarification of plea offer, sentencing range, parole eligibility, and collateral consequences. Consultant will not provide legal advice or engage in strategy discussions.

Confidentiality: All communications and documentation are privileged under attorney-client protection and will not be disclosed outside the defense team without written consent.

Deliverables: Written consultation summary and signed comprehension acknowledgment form.

Fee Structure: [Hourly / Flat rate]

Attorney Signature: ___________________________
Consultant Signature: ___________________________
Date: ___________________________

This simple agreement reinforces your professionalism while protecting all parties from role ambiguity.

Conclusion: Collaboration Creates Competence

Working effectively with attorneys is the cornerstone of a sustainable consulting practice. The consultant's expertise enhances, never replaces, the attorney's work. Through consistent communication, clear boundaries, and meticulous documentation, the consultant becomes an indispensable member of the defense team.

The most successful consultants are not those who speak the loudest, but those who make the attorney's job easier, the client's understanding deeper, and the legal process smoother. Collaboration, professionalism, and discretion transform consulting from a service into a trusted partnership.

Key Takeaways

- Respect professional boundaries: clarify your role early and often.
- Communicate with precision and efficiency; attorneys value clarity.
- All work must flow through counsel to preserve privilege.
- Documentation and professionalism are your best marketing tools.
- Trust is earned through reliability, not persuasion.

Chapter 9: Documentation, Ethics, and Professional Standards

Introduction: Integrity as Infrastructure

Documentation and ethics form the infrastructure of credible sentencing consultation.

No matter how empathetic or experienced a consultant may be, their value collapses without professionalism, accuracy, and accountability.

In the legal world, documentation isn't paperwork, it's **protection**.

Every note, report, and acknowledgment form becomes a safeguard for the client, the attorney, and the consultant.

Ethics, meanwhile, are not simply moral guidelines; they are the invisible contract that earns the trust of the courts and the legal community.

This chapter defines the ethical framework and record-keeping systems that elevate consulting from informal assistance to recognized professional practice.

1. The Purpose of Documentation

A. Legal Protection

Proper documentation provides evidence that:

- The client's understanding was verified and recorded;
- Communication was accurate and timely;
- The consultant acted under the attorney's direction; and
- Confidentiality and ethical boundaries were maintained.

If a dispute arises later; for example, a client claims they were misinformed, documentation becomes your factual shield.

B. Professional Transparency

Attorneys, judges, and potential partners evaluate professionalism through documentation. Organized, consistent records demonstrate:

- Competence
- Accountability
- Reliability

A clean paper trail reflects the consultant's seriousness and reinforces trust.

C. Continuity of Care

In multi-stage cases (pre-plea, sentencing, reentry), clear records ensure consistent information flow across consultations. They also allow attorneys or successor consultants to review prior work without repetition or confusion.

2. Core Ethical Principles

Sentencing consultants operate at the intersection of **law**, **psychology**, and **human service**. That requires a multidisciplinary code of ethics built on five pillars:

1. **Confidentiality:** Protect all privileged communications.
2. **Integrity:** Be honest, accurate, and transparent in every report or discussion.
3. **Competence:** Provide services only within your education and expertise.
4. **Objectivity:** Remain neutral and fact-based in all findings.
5. **Respect:** Uphold the dignity and humanity of every client, regardless of offense.

These principles mirror the **American Bar Association (ABA) Standards for Criminal Justice: Defense Function** §§ 4-3.2 – 4-5.1, which stress candor, loyalty, and diligence in all client interactions.

3. Confidentiality and Privilege

A. Working Under Attorney Direction

To preserve **attorney-client privilege**, consultants must be retained directly by defense counsel or through a written referral agreement.

All work product like notes, reports, or recordings, should be labeled:

"Confidential – Prepared at the Direction of Defense Counsel – Attorney-Client Privileged."

This ensures that your materials are protected from disclosure under Rule 502 of the Federal Rules of Evidence and comparable state statutes.

B. Handling Sensitive Information

Best Practices:

- Store all files on encrypted drives or secure cloud services.
- Use password protection for digital documents.
- Keep physical files in locked cabinets accessible only to authorized personnel.
- Never discuss cases in public or through unsecured communication platforms.

C. Information Release Protocols

If a third party (e.g., probation, treatment provider, or researcher) requests data:

- Obtain written consent from defense counsel **and** the client.
- Release only the specific, necessary information.
- Record the date, purpose, and recipient of every disclosure.

Ethical consultation means **control of information flow**, knowing exactly what leaves your hands and why.

4. Record-Keeping Standards

Consistency in record-keeping defines professionalism. Maintain a uniform system for every case:

A. Mandatory Case File Components

1. Referral Agreement or Authorization Letter
2. Client Intake Form
3. Consultation Summary Report
4. Plea Understanding Form

5. Collateral Consequence Worksheet
6. Confidentiality Acknowledgment
7. Follow-Up Notes or Addenda

B. File Retention Policy

- Keep records for **five years** after case closure unless the attorney requests earlier destruction.
- After the retention period, shred physical copies and permanently delete digital versions.
- Maintain a master index (case number, attorney, dates) without client details for auditing purposes.

C. Documentation Style

- Use objective, factual language.
- Avoid speculative or emotional statements.
- Date and initial all entries.
- Use consistent formatting across all reports.

Example Entry:

09/15/2025 – Client reviewed plea offer; demonstrated understanding of sentencing range and parole eligibility. No questions outstanding. – DRC

5. Professional Conduct and Boundaries

A. Avoiding the Unauthorized Practice of Law (UPL)

Consultants must never:

- Interpret statutes or case law beyond factual explanation;
- Advise clients on whether to plead guilty or go to trial;
- Draft or negotiate plea agreements;

Inside the Sentence

- Represent clients in hearings or legal correspondence.

Safe Boundary Language:

"I can explain what that term means and how it generally works in prison settings, but your attorney will advise you on how it applies to your case."

Maintaining this boundary preserves your role and legal safety.

B. Dual Relationships and Conflicts of Interest

Avoid situations where personal or financial relationships with a client, attorney, or witness could compromise impartiality.

If unavoidable, disclose the potential conflict immediately and defer to counsel's judgment about continued involvement.

C. Professional Presentation

- Dress to match courtroom or law-office standards.
- Use formal, concise communication in emails and reports.
- Be punctual and prepared for all meetings.

Professionalism is your unspoken résumé.

6. Ethical Decision-Making Framework

When facing an ethical dilemma, apply this five-step model:

1. **Identify** the issue: What rule, value, or boundary is at stake?
2. **Consult** with defense counsel or a mentor before acting.
3. **Consider** all consequences (legal, reputational, human).

4. **Choose** the most transparent and least harmful option.
5. **Document** the situation and rationale for your decision.

Example:

If a client discloses new criminal behavior during consultation, note it confidentially and immediately inform defense counsel privately. Do **not** report directly to law enforcement, your duty flows through the attorney.

7. Quality Assurance and Continuous Learning

Ethical excellence requires continual education.
Consultants should stay current on:

- Case law affecting plea and sentencing (*Frye*, *Lafler*, *Padilla*, *Strickland*).
- State sentencing reforms and parole policies.
- Correctional facility procedures and classification changes.
- Trauma-informed and cultural-competence training.
- Professional liability and data-privacy regulations.

Recommended Annual Goals:

- Complete at least **12 hours** of continuing professional development.
- Review and update all templates and forms annually.
- Conduct an internal audit of file security and record retention.

8. Templates and Ethical Clauses

A. Confidentiality Acknowledgment

Confidentiality Statement

I, ____________________, understand that information shared during sentencing consultation is confidential and protected under attorney-client privilege. I agree not to disclose or discuss this information outside the presence or permission of defense counsel.

Client Signature: ____________________ **Date:** ____________
Consultant Signature: ________________ **Date:** ____________

B. Consultant's Ethical Oath

"As a sentencing consultant, I commit to upholding the principles of confidentiality, accuracy, and respect. I will provide services within my professional competence, maintain neutrality, and preserve the dignity of every client I serve."

9. Technology and Data Security

With the digitalization of legal communication, data security is now an ethical requirement, not an option.

Standards for Digital Practice:

- Use encrypted email (TLS 1.2 or higher).
- Employ password managers and two-factor authentication.
- Avoid public Wi-Fi for confidential discussions.
- Regularly update antivirus and system software.
- Use secure video-conferencing platforms (Zoom Pro, MS Teams Gov, or equivalent).

File Naming Protocol Example:

[ClientInitials]_[Case#]_ConsultSummary_[YYYYMMDD].pdf
Consistent naming reduces confusion and supports organized retrieval during audits.

10. Accountability and Reputation

In this profession, *reputation is your credential.*
Adherence to ethics and documentation protocols ensures that when attorneys recommend you, they do so with confidence.

Accountability Practices:

- Keep a written code of conduct signed annually by all staff or contractors.
- Encourage peer review or mentorship among consultants.
- Accept constructive feedback from attorneys.
- If an error occurs, acknowledge it promptly and correct the record.

Transparency is the hallmark of professionalism.

Case Study: Documentation Saves the Defense

Scenario:

Months after a client's sentencing, he files a motion claiming he never understood his plea. The defense attorney produces the consultant's signed "Defendant Plea Understanding Form," the consultation report summarizing the session, and an affidavit verifying comprehension.

Result:

The court dismisses the claim, citing the detailed documentation as evidence that the plea was informed and voluntary.

The consultant's diligence not only protected the attorney but preserved the integrity of the process.

Conclusion: Ethics as Everyday Practice

Ethics and documentation are not separate tasks; they are how the consultant practices every day.

Each form you complete, each word you write, each confidential file you lock contributes to the larger goal of informed justice.

Professional integrity is cumulative: built one report, one ethical choice, one consultation at a time.

When your systems are transparent and your ethics consistent, attorneys trust you, clients respect you, and the justice system benefits from your reliability.

That is the hallmark of a true professional.

Key Takeaways

- Documentation protects clients, attorneys, and consultants alike.
- Work strictly under counsel's direction to preserve privilege.
- Confidentiality, objectivity, and competence are the core ethical pillars.

- Maintain structured file systems and data-security protocols.
- Reputation is earned through consistent ethical conduct and precision.

Chapter 10: Federal vs. State Sentencing—Understanding the Difference

Introduction: Two Systems, One Decision

When a client faces criminal charges, one of the first questions a sentencing consultant must ask is: Is this a state case or a federal case? The answer changes almost everything. Although most collateral consequences associated with being charged and convicted of a felony offense remain, the path through the sentence can be different. Federal and state sentencing operate under fundamentally different frameworks, with different standards, different calculations, different facilities, and a different relationship to parole. A consultant who treats them as interchangeable will quickly lose credibility with experienced defense attorneys.

This chapter provides a structured comparison of the two systems, with practical consulting implications for each. It is not a comprehensive legal analysis which is the attorney's domain but a working guide to understanding how each system functions in practice so that consultants can help clients comprehend the decision in front of them.

The Core Difference: Discretion vs. Guidelines

State sentencing, generally, gives judges meaningful discretion within statutory ranges. A judge may weigh mitigating factors, order probation instead of prison, or impose a sentence below the presumptive range if circumstances warrant. Attorneys negotiate within this space, and sentencing consultants can help clients understand how their individual circumstances might influence the outcome.

Federal sentencing is different. It is governed primarily by the United States Sentencing Guidelines (USSG), a complex point-based system that calculates a recommended sentencing range based on two factors: the offense level (determined by the nature and specifics of the crime) and the criminal history category (determined by prior convictions). The intersection of these two factors on the Sentencing Table produces an advisory guideline range, typically expressed in months.

While the Guidelines have been advisory rather than mandatory since United States v. Booker (2005), federal judges still follow them in the vast majority of cases. Significant departures require written justification and are subject to appellate review. For practical purposes, the Guidelines define the sentence.

The U.S. Sentencing Guidelines: How the Calculation Works

Understanding the Guidelines does not require a law degree, but it does require familiarity with the basic structure. A sentencing consultant working in federal cases should understand the following:

- Base Offense Level: Every federal crime has a base offense level assigned by the Guidelines. Drug offenses, for example, are primarily driven by drug quantity.
- Specific Offense Characteristics: Factors that increase or decrease the offense level. In a drug case, possessing a firearm during the offense adds levels; in a fraud case, the amount of financial loss determines additional levels.

- Adjustments: Role in the offense (leader vs. minor participant), obstruction of justice, acceptance of responsibility. A defendant who accepts responsibility and cooperates may receive a two- or three-level reduction.
- Criminal History Category: Six categories (I through VI) based on the number and severity of prior convictions and their recency. A person with no prior record is Category I; a person with an extensive history may be Category V or VI.
- The Sentencing Table: The intersection of the final offense level and the criminal history category produces a range in months. For example, an offense level of 24 and a criminal history category of II produces an advisory range of 57–71 months.

Consulting Implication: In a federal case, a consultant can help a client understand why the plea is structured the way it is, how the specific offense characteristics apply to their situation, and what the projected guideline range means in practical terms. This is especially valuable when a client is choosing between pleading to one count versus another, as each carries different offense level calculations.

The Pre-Sentence Investigation Report: What It Is and Why It Matters

In the federal system, the sentence does not begin with a judge's decision. It begins with a document. The Pre-Sentence Investigation Report, the PSR, is prepared by the United States Probation Office after a guilty plea or conviction and before sentencing. It is the most consequential document in a federal case that the client has likely never heard of.

The PSR drives the entire federal sentencing calculation. It contains the probation officer's computation of the Guidelines offense level, the criminal history category, and the resulting advisory range. It includes a detailed account of the offense conduct, a summary of the defendant's personal history and characteristics, and a preliminary assessment of the applicable Guidelines. The judge reads it before imposing a sentence. The Bureau of Prisons uses it to determine facility designation and programming needs. It follows the client into the system and shapes decisions that affect their entire sentence.

What the Consultant Needs to Know About the PSR

The consultant does not draft, review, or dispute the PSR; that is the attorney's work. Defense counsel has the right to review the PSR, object to factual inaccuracies, and present arguments against the probation officer's Guidelines calculations. The consultant's role is narrower and more specific: to help the client understand what the PSR is, why it matters, and what the Guidelines range it contains means for their daily life.

Specifically, the consultant should be prepared to:

- Explain that the PSR exists and what it covers; many clients have no idea that a probation officer will investigate and report on their background before sentencing.
- Translate the Guidelines range in the PSR into plain terms: What does a range of 57 to 71 months mean in actual time served under the 85 percent rule, and how does it interact with good conduct time and any applicable FSA credits?
- Help the client understand the criminal history calculation; many clients do not know how prior convictions are scored or why an old conviction is increasing their category.
- Clarify that the judge is not bound by the PSR's Guidelines range but that significant departures require justification, so the range in the PSR is the most likely outcome, not a ceiling or floor.
- Flag any factual inaccuracies the client identifies in the PSR description of the offense and direct them to raise those concerns with the attorney immediately. Factual disputes in the PSR must be addressed before sentencing, not after.

Consulting Implication: The PSR is the document that translates the law into the life. When a consultant helps a client understand the PSR's Guidelines calculation, they close the gap between what the attorney negotiated and what the client will actually experience. That is the work. Leave the legal objections to the attorney, but make sure the client understands what the numbers mean.

Mandatory Minimums: When the Judge's Hands Are Tied

One of the most significant differences between federal and state sentencing is the role of mandatory minimum sentences. Congress has enacted mandatory minimums for a range of federal offenses, most prominently drug trafficking, firearms offenses, and child exploitation crimes.

A mandatory minimum is exactly what it sounds like: a floor below which a judge cannot go, regardless of mitigating circumstances, regardless of the Guidelines, and regardless of the defendant's personal history. The most commonly encountered mandatory minimums in federal drug cases are the 5-year and 10-year minimums tied to drug quantity thresholds under 21 U.S.C. §841.

The only mechanisms that can take a sentence below a mandatory minimum are:

- The Safety Valve (18 U.S.C. §3553(f)): Available to certain first-time, low-level drug offenders who meet specific criteria, including full disclosure of their role in the offense.
- Substantial Assistance (USSG §5K1.1): A motion filed by the government when the defendant has provided substantial

assistance in the investigation or prosecution of others. This is the government's tool, not the defendant's right.

Consulting Implication: A client facing a mandatory minimum must understand that this is not a starting point for negotiation; it is a floor. The consultant's role is to help the client understand what the mandatory minimum means in terms of actual time, what options exist to get below it, and what those options require from the defendant.

No Parole in the Federal System

This is perhaps the single most important structural difference for clients to understand. The federal parole system was abolished by the Sentencing Reform Act of 1984. Federal prisoners do not appear before a parole board. They do not earn their way to early release through good behavior in the same way a state prisoner might.

Instead, federal prisoners serve at least 85 percent of their sentence. The remaining 15 percent can be reduced through good conduct time, but it is capped and does not function like the earned time system described in Chapter 11. What is imposed is, in practical terms, what is served.

For a client comparing a federal plea offer against a state plea offer or weighing federal charges that might be declined in favor of state prosecution, this distinction is enormous. For example, a five-year federal sentence is a minimum of 51 months, whereas a five-year state sentence in a determinate state, with full earned time, ***may*** be approximately 36 months before being eligible for parole.

Consulting Implication: This is one of the most impactful pieces of practical information a consultant can deliver. When a client hears "five years," they need to understand what five years means in the specific system they are entering. The difference between federal and state time is not semantic. It is years of a person's life.

First Step Act Credits: The Other Time Reduction

Good conduct time is not the only mechanism that reduces time served in the federal system. The First Step Act of 2018 created a second, and potentially more significant, time-reduction tool: earned time credits that can move eligible individuals into prerelease custody, a halfway house, or home confinement earlier than the good-conduct time calculation alone would allow.

For eligible clients, First Step Act credits can meaningfully change the answer to the question every client is asking. A consultant who explains only the 85 percent rule without addressing FSA credits is giving the client an incomplete picture.

How FSA Credits Work

Federal prisoners earn FSA credits at a rate of ten days per thirty days of successful participation in approved Evidence-Based Recidivism Reduction (EBRR) programming or Productive Activities (PA). Prisoners assessed as low or minimum risk under the PATTERN risk assessment tool earn fifteen days per thirty days. These credits are not applied against the sentence itself; they are applied toward eligibility for transfer to prerelease custody, either a Residential Reentry Center (halfway house) or home confinement.

To be eligible to apply for FSA credits, a prisoner must:

- Be serving a federal sentence for an eligible offense, certain categories of offense, including most violent offenses and specific drug offenses involving minors, are excluded.

- Not be a deportable non-citizen, individuals subject to a final order of removal are generally ineligible to apply FSA credits toward prerelease custody.
- Have been assessed under the PATTERN tool and not be classified as high or violent risk.
- Have accumulated a sufficient number of credits to cover the transfer period requested.

What This Means in Practice

The practical effect is that an eligible low-risk federal prisoner who participates actively in programming from the beginning of their sentence can transfer to a halfway house significantly earlier than the standard prerelease window would allow, potentially twelve months or more before their projected release date, rather than the standard maximum of twelve months under 18 U.S.C. § 3624(c).

For a client weighing a federal plea offer, the FSA credit calculation is one of the most important pieces of information the consultant can provide, and one of the most frequently omitted. The difference between a client who knows about FSA credits going in and one who discovers them two years into a sentence is the difference between a planned trajectory and a missed opportunity.

The Consultant's Role

The consultant's role regarding FSA credits is to inform, not calculate. The Bureau of Prisons calculates credits through its internal system and applies them based on programming records. The consultant cannot predict with certainty how credits will accumulate or when they will be applied. What the consultant can do is:

- Explain that FSA credits exist and what they can mean for prerelease custody timing.
- Flag whether the client's offense appears to be on the excluded list and direct the attorney to confirm eligibility with federal defense counsel.

- Explain the PATTERN risk assessment and what it measures, so the client understands that their risk score, not just their programming participation, determines the credit rate.
- Make clear that FSA credits require consistent program participation from the beginning of the sentence, and that waiting to engage in programming forfeits credits that cannot be recovered retroactively.
- Flag the deportation bar for any non-citizen client and ensure the attorney has addressed immigration counsel.

Consulting Implication: For an eligible client, the First Step Act changes the calculation in a way that matters. A 63-month sentence for a low-risk, eligible federal prisoner who participates actively in programming may result in transfer to a halfway house substantially earlier than the 85 percent calculation alone suggests. That is information the client needs before they agree to the plea, not after they have already missed two years of programming opportunities.

Federal Facilities: What to Expect

Federal Bureau of Prisons (BOP) facilities differ from state facilities in the designation process, facility types, and program access. Federal facilities are categorized as Minimum (Camps), Low, Medium, High (Penitentiary), and Administrative. Designation is determined by the BOP based on the offense, sentence length, criminal history, and other factors.

Unlike state prison systems, which place individuals convicted on state charges in state-controlled facilities, the BOP, when possible, designates individuals convicted on federal charges to facilities nationwide. For example, a defendant may be sent to a federal facility in a completely different region of the country, far from family and support networks. This is a collateral consequence that is almost never explained at sentencing and that can significantly affect a client's willingness to accept a federal plea.

Consulting Implication: Inform clients about geographic designation early. If being close to family is a priority, this may influence plea strategy. A consultant who raises this issue proactively demonstrates depth of knowledge that an attorney cannot easily replicate.

Comparison Table: Federal vs. State Sentencing—Key Structural Differences

The following summary captures the key structural differences between the two systems for quick reference during consultation. The state column reflects general patterns common across most state systems. Because state rules vary significantly by jurisdiction, consultants should always verify the specific rules that apply to their client's state before presenting any information as fact.

- Sentencing framework: Federal uses the USSG Guidelines + mandatory minimums; most states use statutory ranges with judicial discretion (varies by state).
- Parole: Federal has no parole (85% rule); indeterminate states use a parole board; determinate states use a formula-based release.
- Earned/Good time: Federal caps good conduct time at approximately 15%; state earned time varies widely, from none to 40%+ depending on jurisdiction.
- Facility location: Federal is a nationwide designation; states generally house individuals within their home state when possible.

- Programming requirements: Federal programs vary by facility; state mandatory programming requirements vary by offense type and jurisdiction.
- Post-release supervision: The federal government uses Supervised Release (terms set at sentencing); the states use parole or mandatory supervised release depending on sentencing structure.

Case Study: Federal Time Is Not State Time

Scenario:

A client facing federal drug distribution charges is offered a plea that carries a guidelines range of 63 to 78 months. His family tells him: "That's only five years. You'll be out in two and a half." The defense attorney requests a consultation.

Consultant's Role:

- Corrects the family's misunderstanding directly but respectfully: there is no parole in the federal system. The client will serve a minimum of 85 percent of the sentence imposed.
- Translates the guidelines range into real time: 63 months means approximately 53 months served, not 31.
- Explains the BOP designation process and that the client may be housed at a facility far from family and the home state, a collateral consequence that affects both the client and his support network.
- Addresses the safety valve question with the attorney: the client may be eligible to avoid a mandatory minimum based on his criminal history and role in the offense, but this requires a specific plea structure.

If the client is eligible, the attorney may seek to restructure the plea to preserve safety valve eligibility. The client, now accurately informed, accepts with full understanding of the time he will serve. The family, though disappointed by the reality, is grateful for the clarity. Misunderstanding federal time is one of the most common and consequential errors in sentencing consultation; catching it is one of the most valuable services a consultant can provide.

Conclusion: Know Which System Before You Consult

Every consultation begins with a fundamental question: which system does this case live in? Federal and state sentencing are not variations on a theme. They are structurally different in ways that materially change what a sentence means, how long it lasts, and what options exist for the client.

A sentencing consultant who can explain these differences clearly and translate them into concrete, human terms provides value that cannot be replicated by a legal brief. Attorneys argue the law; consultants illuminate the life. Both systems need that bridge.

Key Takeaways

- Federal sentencing is governed by the U.S. Sentencing Guidelines (USSG); state sentencing typically gives judges more discretion within statutory ranges.
- Federal mandatory minimums create floors that cannot be reduced except through specific mechanisms.
- There is no parole in the federal system; federal prisoners serve a minimum of 85% of their sentence.

- Federal facility designation is nationwide; clients may be housed far from home.
- The same number of years means very different things in federal vs. state custody.

Chapter 11: Consulting with Special Populations

Introduction: Awareness, Not Expertise

Effective sentencing consultation requires the ability to recognize when a client's circumstances place them in a category that demands more than standard practice, and the professional humility to know the limits of what a consultant is qualified to provide.

This chapter addresses five populations that appear regularly in the criminal justice system and that carry specific sentencing implications: youth and juvenile-adjacent clients, clients with mental health diagnoses, clients with substance use disorders, non-English-speaking and limited-English-proficiency clients, and veterans and military-connected clients. Each population requires a different kind of attention from the sentencing consultant.

But this chapter is not a clinical guide. Sentencing consultants are not mental health professionals, immigration attorneys, licensed substance abuse counselors, or veterans' benefits specialists. Presenting yourself as qualified to provide services in those areas when you are not is a professional and ethical failure, one that can harm clients, expose attorneys to liability, and damage the credibility of the consulting field.

What a consultant can and must do is recognize the population, understand how that population's circumstances interact with sentencing exposure and system navigation, adapt communication accordingly, and connect the attorney and client to the right specialist for the work that falls outside the consultant's scope. That coordination function is not a lesser version of consulting. It is one of its most important expressions.

Throughout this chapter, each section closes with a "Know Your Limits" notation identifying the specialist the consultant should be facilitating access to. The consultant's role is to open those doors, not to walk through them alone.

1. Youth and Juvenile-Adjacent Clients

When a young person is charged as an adult, or when a client's offense was committed while they were a minor, the consultant must recognize that both the legal landscape and the communication environment are fundamentally different from a standard adult consultation.

The Supreme Court has established through a series of landmark decisions that youth are constitutionally distinct from adults for sentencing purposes. Roper v. Simmons (2005) prohibited the death penalty for offenses committed by juveniles. Graham v. Florida (2010) prohibited life without parole for non-homicide juvenile offenses. Miller v. Alabama (2012) held that mandatory life without parole for juvenile homicide offenders violates the Eighth Amendment, requiring individualized sentencing consideration. Together, these cases reflect a constitutional recognition that the diminished culpability, greater capacity for change, and developmental differences of young people must be accounted for at sentencing.

For the consultant, this has two practical implications. First, if a client committed their offense as a minor and is serving a lengthy sentence, there may be legal avenues, including post-conviction petitions, sentence modification motions, and parole review mechanisms, that flow directly from these decisions. The attorney needs to know this; the consultant's job is to flag the issue, not to litigate it.

Second, young clients require adapted communication. Abstract time is harder for adolescents and young adults to process meaningfully. Sentence lengths should be translated into concrete terms: age at release, milestones missed, life events that will occur inside versus outside. Family dynamics are often more central than in adult consultations, parents or guardians may be driving decisions, and the consultant must navigate that pressure while keeping the client's own understanding as the priority. Impulsivity, peer influence, and difficulty with long-term thinking are developmental realities, not character flaws, and they require more time, more teach-back, and more patience.

Consulting Implication: Recognize when youth-specific constitutional protections may create legal avenues worth raising with the attorney. Adapt your communication structure for the developmental stage. Do not assume a young client who appears to understand actually does; verify every time.

> **Know Your Limits:** *Refer to juvenile defense specialists, mitigation specialists with adolescent development expertise, and, where applicable, attorneys experienced in post-conviction relief under Miller and its progeny.*

2. Clients with Mental Health Diagnoses

A significant portion of the justice-involved population carries a mental health diagnosis. Depression, anxiety, PTSD, bipolar disorder, schizophrenia, and personality disorders appear at rates substantially higher than in the general population. Intellectual and developmental disabilities are also present at elevated rates. For the consultant, recognizing that a client may be living with one of these conditions is not a clinical task, it is a practical necessity that shapes every aspect of how the consultation is conducted.

The consultant's role is explicitly not diagnostic. You are not qualified to assess, label, or treat any mental health condition, and you should never attempt to do so. What you are qualified to do is observe, adapt, and flag.

Observing means paying attention to signs that a client is struggling to track information, seems disconnected from the conversation, becomes unusually agitated or flat in affect, or cannot consistently recall or restate what has just been discussed. These observations do not tell you what the diagnosis is. They tell you that your standard approach needs to change and that the attorney may need to be aware.

Adapting means adjusting your communication structure: shorter information segments, simpler language, more frequent comprehension checks, and genuine patience with emotional dysregulation. A client who is crying, agitated, or dissociating is not able to receive information in that moment. The consultation may need to pause, to reschedule, or to involve a support person the client trusts.

Flagging means raising competency concerns with the attorney when a client cannot, after multiple careful attempts, consistently restate the basic elements of their charge, the terms of a plea offer, or what accepting the plea means for their life. Competency to stand trial and competency to enter a plea are legal determinations made by courts, but the consultant who observes warning signs and says nothing has failed the client and the attorney both.

Mental health history is also a significant collateral consequence area. A conviction may affect a client's access to community mental health services, their eligibility for certain housing programs, their standing in custody proceedings, and the conditions of any community supervision they receive. These downstream effects require identification and disclosure, in coordination with the attorney.

Consulting Implication: Adapt your communication structure when you observe signs of mental health difficulty. Flag competency concerns to the attorney clearly and promptly. Identify mental health history as a collateral consequence dimension that needs expert attention. Never diagnose, treat, or present yourself as clinically qualified.

> **Know Your Limits:** *Refer to mental health mitigation specialists, forensic psychologists for competency or mitigation evaluations, and clinical social workers with criminal justice experience. For clients with intellectual disabilities, specialists in that area specifically.*

3. Clients with Substance Use Disorders

Active or recently active substance use disorders present a distinct set of challenges for consultation. A client in active addiction may minimize consequences, pursue short-term thinking over long-term planning, and make decisions primarily driven by the desire to return to the community regardless of the wisdom of that choice. A client in early recovery may be emotionally fragile, easily overwhelmed, and uncertain about their own judgment. Neither condition disqualifies a client from receiving a consultation, but both require the consultant to adjust.

The consultant's responsibility is not to address the addiction itself. That work belongs to licensed substance abuse counselors and treatment professionals. What the consultant must do is ensure that the addiction does not prevent the client from making an informed decision about their case.

This means assessing readiness to receive information at the start of each session. A client who is visibly intoxicated or in acute withdrawal cannot meaningfully participate in consultation. Rescheduling is not a failure; it is the professionally correct response. It also means checking with the attorney whether the client has had or should have a clinical assessment, and whether diversion programs, drug courts, or deferred prosecution agreements are available options worth exploring.

The intersection of substance use and sentencing is also a direct consultative topic. Treatment programs may be mandatory conditions of a plea or sentence. Completion of treatment may affect earned time or parole eligibility. Drug courts and diversion programs offer alternatives to incarceration that carry their own requirements and risks. The consultant's job is to ensure the client understands these intersections clearly, not to design a treatment plan.

One important caution: many clients with substance use histories have been through the system before. They may believe they already understand how it works. Prior experience with probation, drug court, or incarceration does not guarantee accurate understanding, it may actually produce overconfidence and resistance to new information. The consultant should not assume prior experience equals prior comprehension.

Consulting Implication: Assess readiness before beginning each session. Identify diversion and treatment options for the attorney's consideration. Explain the sentencing-treatment intersection clearly. Do not assume prior system experience means prior understanding. Never attempt to provide addiction counseling or clinical guidance.

Know Your Limits: *Refer to licensed substance abuse counselors for clinical assessment, drug court coordinators for diversion screening, and, where applicable, attorneys experienced in drug court or deferred prosecution programs.*

4. Non-English-Speaking and Limited-English-Proficiency Clients

Language access is both a constitutional obligation and a practical necessity. A client who does not understand English at a level sufficient to comprehend the terms of a plea, the conditions of a sentence, or the collateral consequences of a conviction has not received effective consultation, regardless of how thorough the consultant's preparation was.

For the sentencing consultant, working with non-English-speaking or limited-English-proficiency clients requires qualified interpretation at every session. This means a professional interpreter, not a family member, not a bilingual friend, not the client's child. Family members and informal interpreters introduce the risk of filtering, softening, or distorting information based on their own emotional response to the situation. A parent who cannot bear to tell their child the full length of a sentence is not a neutral conduit. The consultation requires one.

Beyond language, the consultant must attend to the accuracy of conceptual translation. Many legal terms have no direct equivalent in other languages or legal cultures. "Parole," "deferred judgment," "collateral consequences," and "probation" may carry entirely different meanings, or no meaning at all, in the client's frame of reference. The interpreter's job is to convey the concept accurately, which may require longer explanations than a word-for-word translation allows. The consultant should be prepared for that.

Cultural context matters as well. For clients from countries with very different legal or correctional systems, even basic concepts about how courts work, what a plea means, or what incarceration looks like may need to be built from the ground up. The consultant's job is to recognize that gap and address it, not to assume that a nodding client is a comprehending one.

For non-citizen clients, immigration consequences are a critical and urgent layer that the sentencing consultant must flag but cannot fully address. As established in Padilla v. Kentucky, the duty to inform extends to immigration consequences. A consultant who identifies a non-citizen client and does not immediately ensure that the attorney is addressing immigration exposure, deportation, inadmissibility, loss of lawful status, has missed one of the most consequential aspects of the case. But the analysis of those consequences belongs to an immigration attorney, not the sentencing consultant.

Consulting Implication: Always use a qualified professional interpreter. Verify conceptual translation, not just linguistic translation. Recognize cultural gaps in understanding institutional systems. Flag non-citizen status to the attorney immediately and ensure immigration counsel is involved. Document the interpreter's name, qualifications, and language in every consultation record.

> **Know Your Limits:** *Refer to qualified professional interpreters with legal terminology experience; immigration attorneys for any non-citizen client, this referral is not optional.*

5. Veterans and Military-Connected Clients

Veterans represent a significant portion of the justice-involved population, at rates disproportionate to their share of the general population. Many carry service-connected conditions, PTSD, traumatic brain injury, military sexual trauma, substance use disorders that developed in or after service, that are directly relevant to both culpability and sentencing alternatives. The consultant who does not recognize a veteran client as a veteran is missing one of the most important features of the case.

Veterans Treatment Courts (VTCs) exist in many judicial districts across the United States as a specialized diversion option for veterans charged with criminal offenses. They combine judicial supervision, VA services, peer mentorship from other veterans, and structured accountability into a program that, when completed, often results in charge dismissal or significant sentence reduction. Eligibility requirements vary by jurisdiction, some limit VTCs to veterans with service-connected diagnoses, others are broader, but the consultant's job is to know that this pathway exists, recognize when a client might qualify, and ensure the attorney is exploring it.

For veteran clients who do not qualify for or do not choose VTC, the consultant must still be aware of several distinct areas. VA benefits and their intersection with a conviction require identification: certain offenses can affect access to VA healthcare, disability compensation, housing assistance, and education benefits. These are collateral consequences with real, lasting financial and health implications that must be surfaced in consultation and addressed by a specialist. The consultant identifies them; the veterans' benefits attorney or accredited claims agent analyzes them.

Service history is also a powerful mitigation dimension. A client's combat exposure, documented service-connected diagnoses, and military record can be central elements of a mitigation narrative presented at sentencing. Building that narrative is the work of a mitigation specialist, not the sentencing consultant, but recognizing that the material exists and ensuring the attorney knows it needs to be developed is squarely within the consultant's role.

Finally, communication with veteran clients may require cultural adaptation. Many veterans present as stoic, minimizing difficulty, or resistant to acknowledging vulnerability, particularly around mental health. A client who insists they are "fine" and does not need any "special" programs may be operating from a deeply ingrained cultural norm about strength and self-reliance. The consultant should not read that presentation as an absence of need. It may be exactly the opposite.

Consulting Implication: Identify veteran status at the start of every consultation, ask directly, do not assume. Know whether Veterans Treatment Courts are available in the relevant jurisdiction. Flag VA benefit collateral consequences to the attorney. Recognize military culture's effect on how clients present. Do not attempt to provide trauma treatment or VA benefits analysis.

> **Know Your Limits:** *Refer to veterans Treatment Court coordinators for diversion screening; VA-accredited claims agents or veterans' benefits attorneys for benefit impact analysis; mitigation specialists with military experience for sentencing narratives; VA mental health services or community mental health providers for clinical support.*

Case Study: The Client Who Needed More Than a Consultant

Scenario:

A 41-year-old non-citizen client with limited English proficiency is referred for a sentencing consultation following a felony drug conviction. He has been in the United States for eighteen years, has three U.S.-born children, and owns a small business. His attorney has focused exclusively on the criminal sentence, a likely probation term, and considers the case relatively straightforward.

What the consultant recognizes:

- The client's English is not sufficient for a meaningful consultation without interpretation. The attorney has been communicating through the client's adult daughter, who is present at every meeting.
- The client appears anxious and avoidant during the session, giving short answers and looking to his daughter before responding to any question. The consultant cannot determine whether the client's responses reflect his own understanding or his daughter's filtered version of the questions.
- The client is not a U.S. citizen. A felony drug conviction carries mandatory immigration consequences that have not been discussed.
- The client mentions, in passing, that he has "been nervous and not sleeping well" since his arrest, now eighteen months ago. When asked more, he discloses a history of panic attacks that began before the arrest and have worsened significantly since.

What the consultant does:

- Stops the session and explains to the attorney that the consultation cannot proceed meaningfully without a professional interpreter. The daughter is excused from the interpreter role, respectfully, with explanation.
- A professional interpreter is arranged for the rescheduled session. The consultant verifies that the interpreter has legal terminology experience.
- The consultant flags the immigration exposure to the attorney in writing before the next session: this client is a non-citizen, the charge is a drug felony, and immigration counsel needs to be part of this case immediately.

- The consultant notes the client's reported anxiety history and worsening symptoms in the consultation record and raises it with the attorney as a potential mitigation dimension worth clinical evaluation, not as a diagnosis, but as something that belongs in front of a mental health professional.

Outcome:

Immigration counsel is brought in and identifies that the plea as structured would result in mandatory deportation. The attorney negotiates a modified plea to a different charge that avoids the immigration consequence. A forensic psychologist evaluates the client and produces a report documenting an anxiety disorder that predates the arrest and was exacerbated by the criminal proceedings. Both documents become part of the sentencing presentation. The client receives probation, retains his legal status, and remains with his family and business.

The sentencing consultant did not provide immigration analysis. They did not diagnose or treat anxiety. They recognized what needed to happen, ensured the right specialists were involved, and adapted the consultation to make informed consent possible. That is the full scope of the role, and in this case, it was enough to change the outcome entirely.

Conclusion: The Strength in Knowing Your Limits

The five populations addressed in this chapter are not complications to be managed. They are human realities that the justice system encounters every day and that the sentencing consultant will encounter regularly in practice. Recognizing them, adapting to them, and routing clients toward the right expertise is not a diminished form of consulting. It is a rigorous and honest one.

The consultant who overstates their qualifications, who attempts to provide clinical guidance, immigration analysis, or veterans' benefits counsel without the training to do so, is not serving the client. They are substituting the appearance of comprehensive help for the reality of it, and they are creating risk for the client, the attorney, and themselves.

The consultant who says clearly, "This is what I observed, this is what it means for the consultation, and this is who the attorney needs to bring in," is doing something more valuable: they are functioning as the professional bridge that makes genuinely comprehensive representation possible.

Awareness is expertise. Knowing what you do not know, and knowing who does, is one of the most important things a sentencing consultant can offer.

Key Takeaways

- This chapter addresses recognition and referrals, not clinical practice. Sentencing consultants are not mental health professionals, immigration attorneys, substance abuse counselors, or veterans' benefits specialists.
- Youth clients may benefit from constitutional protections under Roper, Graham, and Miller that create post-conviction legal avenues. Communication must be adapted for developmental stage.
- Mental health diagnoses require adapted communication, careful observation, and prompt flagging of competency concerns to the attorney. Never diagnose or present as clinically qualified.
- Substance use disorders require readiness assessment before each session and clear explanation of treatment-sentencing

intersections. Prior system experience does not equal prior understanding.

- Non-English-speaking clients require professional interpreters, not family members. Non-citizen clients require immigration counsel, this referral is not optional.
- Veteran clients should be screened for Veterans Treatment Court eligibility. VA benefit collateral consequences must be identified and referred to accredited specialists.
- The "Know Your Limits" notation in each section names the specialist the consultant should be facilitating access to. Opening that door is squarely within the consultant's role.
- Knowing what you do not know, and who does, is one of the most important things a sentencing consultant can offer.

Chapter 12: What a Plea Leads To—Understanding Intake, Classification, and Release

Introduction: The Sentence Behind the Sentence

Chapter 3 of this manual established the three pathways a sentence can take: institutional confinement, structured community placement, and conditional community supervision. Chapter 4 established the legal and ethical obligation to explain those pathways in terms a client can genuinely understand before accepting a plea. This chapter addresses the next layer of that obligation, the one most consultants and many attorneys do not reach.

When a client accepts a plea to a term of incarceration, they are not accepting a number. They are accepting entry into a system with its own intake process, its own classification structure, and its own mechanisms for determining when and how they come home. A client who agrees to eight years without understanding what eight years actually involves, how it begins, what controls their daily conditions inside, and what determines their actual release date, has not given the informed consent that Strickland, Frye, Lafler, and Padilla require.

The consultant's job in this chapter is narrow and specific. It is not to train clients to navigate the correctional system, that is the work of Chapter 15. It is to ensure that the attorney, and through the attorney the client, understands enough about how the system operates to make an honest, informed decision about the plea in front of them. Three questions frame that work: What will happen to my client when they first enter the system? What will determine their daily conditions once inside? And what will actually govern when they come home?

1. What Happens at Intake—and Why It Belongs in the Plea Conversation

Every person entering a state prison system in the United States passes through a centralized intake and assessment process before receiving a long-term facility assignment. The names differ by state, Reception and Diagnostic Center, Reception Center, Diagnostic and Evaluation Center, but the function is the same everywhere: the system gathers information, conducts evaluations, and makes the initial decisions that will shape the first years of the sentence.

For the pre-plea consultation, three aspects of intake are directly relevant to the duty to inform.

First, intake takes time, typically two to twelve weeks depending on the state and the individual case. During that period, contact with family is severely restricted. Visitation is typically prohibited or limited to glass visits by appointment. Phone calls are often rationed to once per week. Families who are not told this before sentencing will be blindsided by it. A client who does not know this cannot meaningfully advise their family about what to expect. Explaining the intake timeline is a basic disclosure that belongs in every pre-plea consultation where incarceration is the outcome.

Second, the assessments conducted at intake directly affect the client's conditions of confinement. Medical, mental health, and educational screening results feed into classification decisions that will determine facility placement, housing level, and programming access for months or years. A client with an undisclosed mental health history, an educational deficit that triggers mandatory remedial programming, or a prior institutional record that the system will identify during background review is not entering a neutral process. They are entering a process that will find and act on that information. The attorney and client should know that before the plea is entered.

Third, and most directly relevant to the duty to inform, the intake process produces a risk score. Every state correctional system now uses some form of validated risk and needs assessment instrument. The consultant does not need to know the mechanics of each state's specific tool. What matters for the pre-plea consultation is that this score exists, that it is produced from factors including criminal history, age, education, employment, and prior supervision, and that it will influence classification, programming assignment, and ultimately release decisions. A client who asks "will my past affect how I'm treated in there?" deserves an honest answer: yes, and here is how.

Consulting Implication: Before a plea is accepted, the client and family should know: what the intake process looks like in the relevant state, how long contact will be restricted during that period, that assessments will occur that affect placement and conditions, and that prior history, institutional or otherwise, will be part of the record the system reviews. This is not operational detail for its own sake. It is the information a client needs to make a genuinely informed decision about what they are agreeing to.

2. Classification—Explaining What the Sentence Will Actually Feel Like

One of the most consistent gaps in pre-plea communication is the failure to explain that a sentence of incarceration is not a uniform experience. Two clients sentenced to seven years for similar offenses in the same state may serve those years in dramatically different conditions depending on how the system classifies them. Understanding this, and conveying it honestly to clients, is part of explaining what a plea actually means.

Classification assigns a custody level based on a combination of factors: the risk score from intake assessment, the nature of the offense, any prior institutional history, and specific program or housing needs. Higher classification means more restrictive housing, more limited movement, less programming access, and fewer privileges. Lower classification means more autonomy, greater programming opportunity, and in many systems, access to community corrections facilities that serve as transitional placements before full release. The conditions at a Level 4 facility and the conditions at a Level 2 facility in the same state can be profoundly different, even for clients serving the same sentence length.

Classification is not fixed. It is reassessed periodically, typically annually, and it responds to conduct and program participation. A clean disciplinary record and active program engagement move classification down over time. Serious violations move it up. That relationship between daily behavior and classification level is one of the most important things a client can understand before entering the system, and it is something almost no client knows without being told.

For the pre-plea consultation, the classification discussion has two practical purposes. First, it allows the consultant to give the client a realistic picture of what the sentence will feel like, not just how long it will last. A client agreeing to a plea that will likely result in Level 3 placement should understand what Level 3 conditions involve in the relevant state. A client whose prior institutional record will trigger a higher initial classification should know that before they sign the plea, not after they arrive at the facility. Second, it frames the relationship between daily choices and outcomes in a way that is directly relevant to the client's decision: the sentence is not a fixed experience, and behavior from day one will shape it.

Consulting Implication: Explain classification to every client facing incarceration. Not the mechanics of the instrument the state uses, but the practical reality: the system will assign a level, that level determines daily conditions, and that level responds to behavior and programming over time. If the attorney has reason to believe the client's prior record or offense type will result in a higher initial classification, say so explicitly. Clients who learn this for the first time at intake, rather than before the plea, have not been fully informed.

3. Release—The Question Every Client Is Really Asking

Every client sitting across from a consultant is asking one question underneath all the others: when do I actually come home? The answer to that question depends entirely on the sentencing structure of the state where they were convicted, and it is an answer that belongs in the pre-plea conversation, not delivered in vague terms, but explained with enough specificity that the client understands what they are agreeing to.

State sentencing structures fall into two broad categories that produce very different answers to that question.

In indeterminate sentencing states, the judge imposes a range, five to fifteen years, ten to life, and a parole board holds discretionary authority to release the person at any point after the minimum is served. Release is not guaranteed at the minimum. It is decided by a board that weighs the institutional record, risk assessment scores, release planning, and in many states, victim input. The client serving an indeterminate sentence does not have a fixed release date. They have an eligibility date and a process, one that can grant release or deny it based on how the sentence has been served.

In determinate sentencing states, the judge imposes a fixed term, and release is governed by a formula: the sentence, minus good time credits earned through clean conduct, minus any additional earned time credits accumulated through program participation. The release date is, in principle, calculable from the moment of sentencing. At least seventeen states have abolished or severely curtailed discretionary parole, relying instead on these formula-based mechanisms. In these states, the client who understands the earned time calculation before entering the system can see, concretely, what a disciplinary violation costs them and what completing a program earns them.

The federal system operates under its own distinct framework, addressed in Chapter 12. In brief: there is no parole for federal offenses committed after November 1, 1987. Federal prisoners serve at minimum 85 percent of their sentence. Good conduct time of up to 54 days per year is available, and the First Step Act created an additional system of earned time credits for participation in approved programs that can accelerate transfer to prerelease custody or supervised release. The federal system rewards program participation in a direct, calculable way, and explaining that to a client before they enter it is a basic duty.

Beyond the primary release mechanism, the consultant should be aware of several additional pathways that may be relevant depending on the client and the jurisdiction: compassionate and medical release for individuals with serious health conditions; executive clemency, available through the governor in every state and through the President federally; and second-look provisions, which allow courts or parole boards in a growing number of states to review long sentences after a defined period. None of these is a routine release mechanism, but each is real, and for clients facing long sentences, they may be the most relevant pathway the attorney should be researching.

Consulting Implication: The release question must be answered before the plea is signed, not after. The consultant should be able to tell the client, in plain terms, which release mechanism governs their sentence, what it requires, and what a realistic timeline looks like given the sentence being offered. For clients in indeterminate states, that means explaining the parole process honestly, including the reality that parole is discretionary and not guaranteed at the minimum. For clients in determinate states, that means explaining the good time and earned time formula so the client understands both the potential reduction and the cost of misconduct. Vague assurances that "you could get out early for good behavior" are not sufficient disclosure.

4. The Consultant's Reference: Release Mechanisms by System Type

The following table is designed as a quick reference for consultants preparing a pre-plea consultation. It frames each release dimension around the questions clients actually ask. Because state rules vary and change, consultants should always verify the specific rules for the jurisdiction where their client was sentenced.

Questions the client may ask	Indeterminate states	Determinate states	Federal (BOP)
"When can I get out early?"	Parole board decides after minimum served	Formula: sentence minus good time / earned time	No parole; good conduct time + First Step Act credits

"What controls my release date?"	Parole board discretion + institutional record	Conduct and program participation	PATTERN risk score + program credits
"How much could I reduce my sentence?"	Varies; no guaranteed formula	Calculable from sentencing day	Up to 54 days/yr good time; FSA credits vary
"What happens after I'm released?"	Parole supervision (length varies)	Mandatory supervised release in most states	Supervised release term set at sentencing
"Who decides if I stay or go?"	Parole board (political, discretionary)	Math — with conduct and programming variables	BOP + First Step Act eligibility rules

5. Putting It Together: What the Pre-Plea Conversation Covers

The information in this chapter is not background knowledge for the consultant alone. It is disclosure material that belongs in the pre-plea conversation, explained in plain language, verified through teach-back, and documented in the consultation record.

A client accepting a plea to incarceration should leave the consultation understanding the following four things, all of which flow directly from this chapter.

What the first weeks will look like. The client should know that they will enter an intake facility, that this process takes time, that family contact will be limited during that period, and that assessments will occur that affect their placement. The name of the intake facility in the relevant state, the approximate timeline, and what the family should expect during that period are all appropriate to include.

What their daily conditions will be determined by. The client should understand that classification, not just sentence length, shapes what incarceration actually feels like, that classification is based on identifiable factors some of which apply to them specifically, and that it responds to their conduct and program engagement from the first day. If the attorney knows or suspects that the client's profile will result in a higher initial classification, that should be communicated honestly before the plea is entered.

What will govern their release date. The client should be able to answer, in their own words, which release mechanism applies to their sentence and what it requires. An indeterminate sentence means parole eligibility at the minimum, with discretionary board review. A determinate sentence means a formula that the client can see and that they have some agency over. The federal system means 85 percent of the sentence with specific credit mechanisms. The client who cannot restate this after the consultation has not been informed, they have been spoken at.

What their behavior inside has to do with coming home. This is the connection that most clients do not grasp without explicit explanation. In indeterminate states, the parole board will review the institutional record. In determinate states, disciplinary violations cost earned time in measurable increments. In both systems, program participation builds the record that will matter most when release decisions are made. The client who understands this before they enter the system is not the same as the client who discovers it after their first violation.

Consulting Implication: Documentation of this conversation belongs in the consultation record. Note that the release mechanism was explained, that the client was able to restate it, and that the connection between daily conduct and release timing was discussed. This is not bureaucratic formality. It is evidence that the duty to inform was actually fulfilled, the same evidence that protects the attorney and the consultant if questions arise later about the quality of the advice the client received.

Case Study: The Plea the Client Thought She Understood

Scenario:

A 34-year-old woman is offered a plea to six years in a determinate sentencing state with an earned time credit system. Her attorney explains the sentence length, the likely facility, and the fact that she may be able to "get out early for good behavior." The client accepts the plea. No sentencing consultant is involved. She enters the system two weeks after sentencing.

What she did not know:

- The state offers earned time credits of up to eight days per month for program participation. Over six years, maximum credits would reduce her sentence by nearly sixteen months. She has no plan to pursue programming. She does not know this calculation exists.
- Her prior misdemeanor record and her educational history, she did not complete high school, will affect her initial classification and trigger mandatory remedial programming at intake, extending the intake period by several weeks beyond what she expected.
- Family contact during intake will be limited to one phone call per week. Her two children, ages nine and eleven, will not be able to visit for the first six weeks. No one told her family this.

Her sister drives four hours to the facility two weeks after sentencing and is turned away.

- In this state, a single Class I disciplinary violation forfeits 90 days of accumulated good time. Eight months into her sentence, she gets into a verbal altercation that escalates and is classified as a Class I. She loses the credits she has built. She will not know, until it happens, what that cost her.

What a pre-plea consultation would have covered:

- The intake timeline and contact restrictions, so her family was prepared and the children's first weeks without her were not compounded by a failed visit.
- The earned time calculation, specifically, what sixteen months of potential reduction looks like against a six-year sentence, and what a Class I violation costs against that number.
- The fact that her educational history would trigger mandatory programming at intake, framed not as a problem but as a starting point, and connected to the earned time system: completing the GED program earns credits.
- An honest explanation of what "good behavior" actually means in a determinate state, not a vague promise, but a specific formula she could hold onto.

What this illustrates:

The attorney in this case was not negligent in the conventional sense. The plea was sound. The sentence was appropriate. But the client did not understand what she was agreeing to in any operational sense, and the gap between what she understood and what was true shaped the experience of her entire sentence. That gap is precisely what the duty to inform is designed to close. It is precisely what a sentencing consultant is there to fill.

Conclusion: Informed Consent Requires Operational Honesty

The duty to inform established by Strickland, Frye, Lafler, and Padilla requires that clients understand the consequences of their plea. The plea checklist in Chapter 4 establishes what that means at the legal level. This chapter establishes what it means at the operational level: a client has not been fully informed if they do not know what happens to them when they walk through the intake door, what will determine their daily conditions inside, and what will govern when they come home.

None of this requires the consultant to be a correctional expert. It requires them to understand the structure well enough to explain it honestly, in terms the client can absorb and restate. The intake process, the classification system, and the release mechanism are not institutional trivia. They are the operational content of the sentence the client is being asked to accept. Explaining them is part of the work.

Key Takeaways

- A client accepting a plea to incarceration is not accepting a number. They are accepting entry into a system with a specific intake process, classification structure, and release mechanism. All three belong in the pre-plea conversation.
- Intake involves a period of restricted family contact, typically two to twelve weeks, during which assessments occur that directly affect classification and conditions. Clients and families should be told this before sentencing.
- Classification determines the daily reality of incarceration. It is driven by identifiable factors, it is reassessed periodically, and it responds to conduct and program participation. Clients should understand this before they agree to a plea.

- Release mechanisms differ fundamentally between indeterminate states (parole board discretion), determinate states (formula-based good time and earned time), and the federal system (no parole; good conduct time and First Step Act credits). The applicable mechanism must be explained specifically, not vaguely.
- The connection between daily conduct and release timing is the most important operational disclosure a consultant can make. Disciplinary violations cost earned time in measurable increments. Program participation builds the record that parole boards and release formulas respond to.
- Document the release mechanism conversation in the consultation record. The client should be able to restate which mechanism governs their sentence and what it requires. If they cannot, the information has not been received.

Chapter 13: Building a Path—Navigating Incarceration with Purpose

Introduction: What the Sentence Doesn't Tell You

A sentence is, on its face, a number. Twenty years. Five to fifteen. Life with the possibility of parole. Defendants and their families hear the number and carry it home like a stone, imagining only the weight of it, the years, the absence, the waiting.

What the sentence does not tell you is that inside that number lives an entire architecture of choices. It does not tell you that how a person enters the system, what they do in the first weeks, which programs they pursue, how they conduct themselves on the unit, and how they engage with staff and administration will shape not only the quality of those years, but often the length of them. It does not tell you that early release mechanisms may exist, that programming can alter classification and opportunity, or that the record built inside will one day speak in parole hearings, clemency petitions, employment interviews, and reentry itself.

This is the chapter most sentencing consultants may not think they should deliver. The legal duty to inform, addressed throughout this manual, covers the plea, the sentence, and the collateral consequences. But any consultant serious about serving the whole person must go one step further: explaining what it actually means to navigate a sentence with intention.

This chapter is that explanation. It is not theory. It is drawn from decades of lived experience inside the Colorado Department of Corrections, from programs that changed lives, from educational paths that opened doors incarceration was supposed to close, and from the hard-won understanding that the consultant's job does not end when the gavel falls. For many clients, that is where the real work begins.

1. The Mindset That Changes Everything

Among the most decisive factors within a client's control is the mindset they bring into incarceration. Facility placement matters. Sentence length matters. Classification matters. Mental health, age, history, and institutional culture all matter. But within those realities, mindset often determines whether a person is merely carried by the system or begins, deliberately, to build something inside it.

That decision sounds simple. Inside a correctional institution, it is not. The environment is often structured in ways that erode agency. The culture of incarceration, the convict code, the pull of negative associations, and the daily pressure to adapt to the institution on its own terms all work against intentional change. Many people who enter prison are absorbed by that culture rather than navigating through it with purpose.

A consultant's role is to name that reality before the client walks through the door. The conversation does not need to be dramatic, but it must be honest. The first question is not whether the system is fair. It is not whether the sentence is excessive. It is not whether the coming years will be hard. The first question is simpler and more consequential: What will you do with the time you have?

That question frames the entire sentence. The client who treats incarceration only as punishment will likely experience it one way. The client who treats it as a period of preparation, however painful or unwanted, opens the possibility of a different outcome. This mindset does not romanticize prison. It does not deny harm, grief, or loss. It simply refuses to surrender authorship.

Programs such as *The 7 Habits of Highly Effective People* offer a useful framework for that orientation. Focus on the circle of influence rather than the circle of concern. Choose response over reaction. Begin with an end in mind. Consultants do not need to teach these programs themselves. But they should know they exist, name them to clients, and help frame incarceration as a period in which daily decisions still matter.

The client who understands mindset as a survival strategy, a discipline, and a pathway home is more likely to do the work this chapter describes.

Consulting Implication: Before a client enters any correctional facility, they should leave the consultation understanding two things clearly: first, that positive opportunities inside exist but will not be handed to them; and second, that the path through a sentence begins with a decision they must renew daily.

2. The First Ninety Days: Classification, Reputation, and the Choices That Echo

If mindset sets the frame, the first ninety days test it.

The opening phase of a sentence is among the most consequential periods of the entire term. It affects classification, housing, facility placement, programming access, and social positioning. Consultants who do not prepare clients for this period are sending them into the most formative stretch of incarceration without a map.

Newly sentenced individuals typically enter through the state's reception and diagnostic center, where intake and classification decisions shape initial placement. The institution begins assessing the client immediately. Risk level, offense history, program needs, demeanor, disciplinary behavior, and institutional adjustment all begin forming a record from the start.

That early record matters. Formal write-ups can affect classification, housing, programming eligibility, and earned time. A serious disciplinary issue in the first months can follow a client for years, closing doors that would otherwise have opened. A poor start is not always permanent, but it can be costly.

The social dimension is equally important. In those first weeks, a new arrival is being read by everyone around them. Their demeanor, affiliations, reactions, and apparent intentions are all being assessed. The choices they make about who to associate with, what conflicts to step around, and how to carry themselves will influence the reputation that follows them through the sentence.

This is not abstract advice. It is practical counsel. The client who arrives understanding how intake works, what classification means, how easily a reputation is formed, and how closely daily behavior is tied to future opportunity is better positioned than the client who enters blind.

Consulting Implication: Walk clients through the intake process before they enter. Explain classification, explain what can damage it, explain the social realities of the first weeks, and explain that a strong beginning creates options. Clients need specifics here, not general encouragement.

3. Programming: The Architecture of a Productive Sentence

Once the client is oriented and stabilized, the next question is engagement.

Most correctional systems, though not equally across facilities, contain a landscape of programs, classes, treatment tracks, and structured activities that many defendants know nothing about before they enter. Some are required. Many are voluntary. All of them have significance beyond their curriculum.

Programming matters first because it affects institutional opportunity. Participation often improves access to lower classification over time, greater privileges, expanded work opportunities, and additional programs. It signals that the client is not simply serving time passively.

Programming also matters because it creates documentary evidence of effort and change. Cognitive programs, substance abuse treatment, life skills classes, vocational certifications, restorative justice work, mental health tracks, faith-based initiatives, and reentry programs all become part of the institutional record. They show pattern, consistency, and direction.

Programming matters as well for future review. Whether the issue is parole, clemency, sentence modification, or reentry planning, decision-makers look for evidence that the person used the sentence constructively. Completed programs do not prove transformation by themselves. But the absence of engagement often speaks just as loudly.

In many correctional settings, some programs do more than transmit information. They create peer cultures of accountability, leadership, and support. A person who completes a meaningful program and later facilitates it for others is not merely checking a box. They are assuming a different role inside the institution.

The consultant's task is not to promise access where access may be limited. Availability varies by facility, jurisdiction, waitlist, staffing, and security level. The task is to ensure the client understands the categories of opportunity that may exist, why they matter, and why passive time is almost always wasted time.

Consulting Implication: Help clients build an informal program plan before they enter. What should they pursue first? What comes next? What records should they keep? A client who enters with a sequence in mind has already begun building direction.

4. Education: The Most Powerful Tool Available

Of all the paths available inside, education remains the most durable.

The research consistently shows that educational attainment during incarceration is associated with stronger reentry outcomes, lower recidivism, and better long-term stability. But even apart from research, the practical value is obvious. Education builds something portable. A credential leaves the facility with the client. It continues to speak after release.

The educational path may begin with literacy or a GED. From there it may move to vocational training, certificates, associate's degrees, bachelor's degrees, and, in some cases, graduate education. Expanded Pell eligibility and other correctional education initiatives have widened access in many places, though access remains uneven and often depends on facility, funding, and institutional support.

Where internal college programming is unavailable, correspondence study and independent education may still provide a path forward. The form may vary. The value does not.

Education does more than improve employability. It changes identity. A paralegal certificate can build legal literacy. An associate's degree can demonstrate discipline and sustained effort. A bachelor's degree can lay the foundation for professional work and self-sufficiency. A graduate degree completed under severe institutional limitations demonstrates not only intelligence, but endurance, structure, and will.

Just as important, education interrupts the story a client may be telling themselves. Many enter prison convinced that school is not for them, that they are too far behind, too old, too damaged, or too disconnected from academic life to succeed. That belief costs people years.

The consultant who plants the possibility of education before the sentence begins is planting something that can grow for the duration of the term. The GED pursued in year one may become the associate's degree in year three, the bachelor's degree in year six, and something more after that. Each success expands the next.

Consulting Implication: Ask every client directly about their educational history. Then help them see education inside not as an abstract virtue, but as one of the clearest ways to leave with proof of growth, skill, and readiness.

5. Work, Routine, and the Structure That Sustains

That matters more than many people realize.

Work assignments, study time, physical activity, reading, writing, and simple consistency form the structure that keeps a sentence from collapsing into drift. Kitchen work, laundry, recreation, library assignments, tutoring roles, vocational shops, orderly positions, and other institutional jobs may not look glamorous from the outside. Inside, they can become part of a disciplined life.

The value is not only the assignment itself. It is the habits the assignment demands. Showing up. Following through. Being reliable. Managing time. Doing work well even when the work feels small. Those habits are visible to staff and case managers, but more importantly, they reshape the client from the inside out.

Routine also stabilizes the mind. Exercise, reading, study, and consistent daily structure are not luxuries in prison. They are anchors. In an environment defined by disruption, tension, and institutional control, self-imposed discipline can preserve mental clarity and direction.

This section should not be overstated. Routine alone is not transformation. A work assignment alone does not outweigh serious disciplinary problems or a lack of engagement elsewhere. But routine is often the platform on which everything else rests. Without it, larger goals rarely hold.

Consulting Implication: Encourage clients to approach even ordinary work and daily habits as part of sentence management. The question is not whether the assignment looks important. The question is whether the client can use it to build consistency.

6. Earned Time, Good Time, and the Mechanics of Early Release

Clients need to understand, precisely, how time can be reduced where the law allows it. They need to understand the difference between sentence length on paper and time actually served in practice. And they need to understand how quickly poor decisions can destroy progress.

In Colorado, for example, earned time may allow incarcerated individuals to reduce the period they actually serve through a combination of good conduct and program participation. The details must always be verified against the governing statutes, policies, offense type, and sentence structure in the client's case. But the central consulting point remains the same: release is often shaped not just by the sentence imposed, but by conduct during service of that sentence.

In other jurisdictions, good time and earned time are structured differently. In the federal system, for example, good conduct time and First Step Act time credits operate under their own rules and eligibility limits. Consultants handling federal matters must know those mechanics with precision, not approximation.

This is one of the places where legal language must be translated into plain language. The client needs to see the math. They need to understand what sustained compliance can yield, what program participation may add, and what a serious disciplinary violation can cost. A year of disciplined behavior can be lost far faster than it is built.

Other release-related mechanisms may also matter depending on the jurisdiction: parole eligibility, compassionate release, sentence modification, medical release, executive clemency, prerelease custody, supervised release, or community-based transitions. Each has its own standards. But nearly all of them are shaped, directly or indirectly, by the institutional record.

The consultant's job is to connect the abstract number imposed at sentencing to the lived choices that affect when the door actually opens.

Consulting Implication: Build release mechanics into the consultation explicitly. Show the client what maximum compliance could mean. Then show them what a serious violation could cost. A client who understands that relationship is more likely to protect their future when pressure comes.

7. Avoiding the Pitfalls: The Most Common Mistakes and How to Prevent Them

A productive sentence is not built by good intentions alone. It is also protected by the avoidance of predictable dangers.

Certain patterns derail people again and again across institutions and jurisdictions. These are not hypothetical risks. They are the recurring traps of incarceration.

The first is gang or group involvement. For many new arrivals, organized groups offer belonging, identity, and protection. The price is submission to a code that tends to pull the person toward conflict, contraband, politics, and violence. What begins as alignment for safety often becomes an obligation that reshapes the sentence in destructive ways.

The second is substance abuse. Drugs circulate through nearly every correctional system regardless of security level. For clients with a prior history of addiction, the threat is obvious. For others, prison itself can become the setting in which substance use escalates. Either way, addiction destabilizes routine, destroys eligibility, increases discipline, and makes intentional progress difficult to sustain.

The third is unmanaged conflict. Correctional facilities compress tension. Disrespect, perceived disrespect, debt, frustration, and interpersonal friction are part of daily life. The client who cannot de-escalate, walk away, or think beyond the moment will often pay a steep price for that limitation.

The fourth is isolation. Some clients attempt to solve the dangers above by withdrawing from everything. But total withdrawal often leads to its own problems: no programming, no support, no structure, deteriorating mental health, and no positive institutional footprint. The answer is not passive isolation. It is selective, intentional engagement.

Clients do not need fear-based lectures. They need honest naming of the terrain. The more clearly they understand the recurring traps before they encounter them, the more likely they are to recognize them in real time.

Consulting Implication: Discuss these pitfalls directly in every incarceration consultation. Not as moral failures, but as foreseeable risks that require a plan.

8. Family, Support Systems, and the Relationships That Sustain

Institutional progress does not happen in a vacuum. The strongest internal path is easier to maintain when it is reinforced from outside.

Family and community support are not sentimental extras. They are structural components of sentence navigation and reentry success. The client who remains connected to healthy support systems generally enters release with more stability, more accountability, and more reason to protect what has been built.

Maintaining those relationships is difficult. Communication costs money. Visits require travel, time, and coordination. Years of incarceration place emotional strain on everyone involved. Still, the effort matters. Letters, calls, consistent honesty, and visible progress help preserve ties that might otherwise fracture under the weight of absence.

Families also need guidance. Support is not the same as enabling. A helpful family member reinforces education, treatment, routine, accountability, and lawful preparation for release. A harmful dynamic introduces chaos, manipulation, unrealistic expectations, or institutional risk. Consultants who can speak to both the client and the family add real value here.

For clients with children, the issue becomes even more urgent. Parenting through incarceration requires intention. Age-appropriate honesty, consistency of contact, and participation in parenting or family-strengthening programs can preserve bonds that would otherwise erode over time. Those bonds matter both to the child and to the parent's reentry trajectory.

This section belongs here because family is not merely an emotional support at the edge of the sentence. It is part of what sustains discipline across the years and part of what gives reentry somewhere to land.

Consulting Implication: Ask every client who is in their corner, who can remain consistent, and what those people need to understand in order to help well. The support plan is part of the sentence plan.

9. The Record You Build Is the Case You Present

Every year of incarceration builds a record. That record will become the most important document in nearly every future proceeding that matters. It will be read by parole boards, clemency reviewers, case managers, employers, housing providers, community partners, and sometimes courts. Long before the client speaks for themselves, the record will speak for them.

For parole, the record shows whether the client used the sentence productively. For clemency, it demonstrates whether change has been sustained, documented, and credible over time. For reentry, it becomes the backbone of the story the client must tell about who they are now and what they did with the years they were given.

This is why programming, education, discipline, work history, treatment participation, mentorship, leadership, and family stability all matter. They are not isolated achievements. They are components of a cumulative narrative.

The petition may frame the argument. The hearing may provide the moment. But the record is the substance.

That truth should be explained early. It should not wait until the eve of parole, the filing of a clemency application, or the final year before release. By then, the record is largely built.

Consulting Implication: Tell clients plainly that incarceration is not a pause in their story. It is a chapter that is writing evidence every day. The only real question is what that evidence will show.

Case Study: Thirty Years to Purpose

A client in his early twenties is sentenced to life without the possibility of parole on a first-degree murder conviction under a complicity theory. He did not pull the trigger. The trigger man pleads to a lesser charge. He does not accept the sentence. He fights through the courts for years and loses at every level.

At his lowest point, after agreeing to hear his case, the Colorado State Supreme Court denies his petition for certiorari, he turns to heroin. He rises in the prison social hierarchy, becomes a gang leader, and spends years at the intersection of contraband, violence, and the convict code. From the outside, his sentence appears consumed by the institution.

The Turn

In his mid-thirties, in segregation in one of Colorado's most restrictive facilities, something changes. He decides the life he has been living is not the life he intends to finish. He begins stepping away from the role that had defined him. He begins again.

The Path

He completes The 7 Habits of Highly Effective People, then becomes a facilitator. He earns a paralegal certificate through correspondence study. He completes an associate's degree in paralegal studies with a 3.9 GPA. He works in the prison K-9 program, training rescue dogs and learning patience, consistency, and empathy in the process. He earns sobriety and keeps it.

He then earns a Bachelor of Science in Business Administration. During the COVID-19 lockdown, with no word processor or library access, he handwrites MBA papers in APA format, mails them out, and completes a Master of Business Administration degree.

He becomes a facilitator for The Power of Consistency. He completes Mental Health Peer Assistant training. He is elected to the Legislation on the Inside program and helps co-author legislation that passes both chambers of the Colorado General Assembly. He is hired by Adams State University as an adjunct professor, becoming the first incarcerated person in the nation hired by a university as a college faculty member.

After almost thirty-one years, Governor Jared Polis grants him clemency. He is released on January 31, 2024.

The Lesson:

This case study is not presented as a guarantee. It is presented as proof of what is structurally possible when a person commits to building a path rather than merely serving a sentence.

The opportunities were not unlimited. They were not evenly distributed. They were not handed over. But programming existed.

Education existed. Record-building existed. Pathways to earned time, reduced custody, clemency, and release existed. What turned possibility into outcome was sustained decision-making over time.

That is the lesson for the consultant. The goal is not to tell every client they will replicate this result. The goal is to help every client understand that the sentence contains choices, that those choices accumulate, and that the path begins on day one.

Conclusion: The Sentence Is Not the End of the Story

The work of a sentencing consultant does not end at the plea hearing or at sentencing. For clients facing incarceration, one of the most important consultations may be the one that happens after the sentence is imposed, when the client and family are still in shock and have not yet begun to understand what the coming years will actually require.

That is what this chapter is meant to provide.

The path through incarceration with purpose is real. So are the risks. So are the mechanics. Programming matters. Education matters. Discipline matters. Family support matters. The record built inside matters. The person who exits with sobriety, credentials, structure, and a documented history of effort leaves with a fundamentally different foundation than the person who does not.

The sentence is not the end of the story. It is a chapter in it. And that chapter is not written by the number alone. It is written by the choices that follow.

Help your clients understand that. Then help them plan.

Key Takeaways

- The mindset a client brings into incarceration is one of the most powerful factors within their control. Prepare them to enter with intention.
- The first ninety days shape classification, reputation, and trajectory. Clients should be prepared for that period specifically and concretely.
- Programming is not filler. It creates opportunity, documents effort, and strengthens every future case for release or reentry.
- Education is the most durable asset a client can carry out of a correctional facility. Plant that ambition early.
- Work, routine, and daily discipline create the structure that sustains long-term progress.
- Earned time, good time, and other release mechanisms must be explained precisely. Clients need to understand both the benefits of compliance and the cost of misconduct.
- Gang involvement, substance abuse, unmanaged conflict, and isolation are recurring threats to a productive sentence and should be named in advance.
- Family and community support are not peripheral. They are part of both sentence navigation and reentry success.
- The institutional record built during incarceration becomes the case the client will one day present to parole boards, clemency reviewers, employers, and the world outside.
- The consultant's role does not end at sentencing. For many clients, the most meaningful guidance begins the day after the gavel falls.

Chapter 14: Building a Sentencing Consulting Business

Introduction: From Expertise to Enterprise

A sentencing consultant's work is more than service; it's a calling grounded in purpose. But purpose without structure is fragile.

To bring your impact to scale, you must translate personal expertise into a sustainable, ethical business model that communicates value, attracts clients, and maintains credibility within the legal profession.

This chapter provides the blueprint for doing just that, developing a business that is both **mission-driven** and **professionally sound**, rooted in the same principles of transparency, accountability, and structure that define effective consultation.

1. Defining Your Mission and Value Proposition

Your **mission statement** should express not only what you do, but *why* you do it.

A strong mission guides decisions, inspires trust, and distinguishes your practice in a specialized market.

Example Mission Statement:

"To empower attorneys and their clients through informed sentencing consultation, bridging the gap between legal procedure and human understanding while upholding the highest ethical standards of clarity, compassion, and professionalism."

Your **value proposition** communicates the tangible benefits you bring to law firms and their clients. It should answer one question:

> *Why should an attorney hire you instead of managing the process alone?*

Example Value Proposition:

"I help attorneys reduce risk of post-conviction claims, enhance client comprehension, and strengthen defense integrity by providing clear, documented sentencing consultation based on lived experience, legal knowledge, and professional ethics."

When attorneys understand your *value to their practice*, they see your service not as an expense, but as an investment in client satisfaction and legal protection.

2. Building the Framework: Business Formation and Structure

A. Legal Structure

Choose a legal entity that balances flexibility, liability protection, and credibility:

- **Limited Liability Company (LLC):** Ideal for independent consultants seeking personal liability protection.
- **Professional Corporation (PC):** Appropriate if employing licensed professionals or forming a team.
- **Sole Proprietorship:** Simplest, but offers no liability shield.

Consult a business attorney or CPA for formation filings and operating agreements.

B. Business Essentials

- Obtain a **federal EIN** (Employer Identification Number) for tax purposes.
- Register your business name with your Secretary of State.
- Secure professional **liability insurance** (errors and omissions coverage).
- Establish a dedicated **business bank account** and accounting system (QuickBooks, Wave, or FreshBooks).
- Develop **written service contracts** for all engagements.

These basics transform your work from a freelance activity into a formal enterprise that attorneys can confidently retain.

C. Professional Liability Insurance

Professional liability insurance, also called errors and omissions (E&O) insurance, is not optional for a practicing sentencing consultant. It is a professional baseline.

You are producing documentation used in legal proceedings. You are advising attorneys on matters that bear directly on whether a client's plea is legally defensible as informed and voluntary. If a client later claims that your consultation was deficient, that you misinformed them, failed to disclose a consequence, or produced a record that misrepresented their understanding, you need coverage. Without it, you are personally exposed to any claim made against your work.

What to Look For

- **Coverage amount:** A minimum of $1 million per occurrence / $2 million aggregate is standard for legal support professionals.

Some attorneys will require you to carry this level of coverage before retaining you.
- Policy type: Most E&O policies are claims-made, meaning coverage applies when the claim is filed, not when the work was done. Ensure your policy includes tail coverage if you ever stop practicing.
- Scope of coverage: Verify that the policy covers your specific work, sentencing consultation, documentation, and educational services. General business liability does not cover professional errors.
- Cost: E&O insurance for legal support professionals typically runs $500–$1,500 per year, depending on coverage limits and business volume. This is a deductible business expense.

Contact a business insurance broker specializing in legal support professionals. Professional associations in the consulting and legal support space often maintain lists of recommended carriers.

Consulting Implication: Carrying professional liability insurance is also a marketing asset. When an attorney asks whether you are insured, and many will, the answer "yes, I carry E&O coverage at $1 million per occurrence" signals that you operate at a professional level. It removes a barrier to engagement and demonstrates that you take your accountability as seriously as you take your work.

3. Core Services and Offerings

Your consulting business should provide a range of structured, clearly defined services. Each offering should have its own process, deliverables, and pricing tier.

Primary Services

1. **Plea and Sentencing Consultation**

- One-on-one or remote sessions with defendants (through counsel).
- Deliverable: Consultation Summary + Plea Understanding Form.

2. **Collateral Consequence Analysis**
   - Written breakdown of likely collateral effects by conviction type.
   - Deliverable: Collateral Consequence Worksheet (customized per jurisdiction).
3. **Attorney Support and Documentation**
   - Drafting comprehension records, acknowledgment forms, and client education materials.
   - Deliverable: Ready-to-file forms and summaries for attorney files.
4. **Educational Workshops and CLEs**
   - Seminars for public defenders, private attorneys, or law students.
   - Deliverable: Presentation slides, materials, and certificates of completion.
5. **Expert Testimony or Mitigation Support (Advanced)**
   - Contextual testimony about prison environments, parole, or rehabilitation programming.
   - Deliverable: Expert report or affidavit under attorney direction.

Consulting Insight Box:

Clarity of service equals clarity of value. When attorneys know exactly what you deliver, and how it protects their work, they become long-term partners, not one-time clients.

4. Pricing Models and Revenue Streams

Pricing should reflect the complexity of the work, your professional background, and market demand.
Avoid underpricing; your value lies in risk reduction, not hourly labor.

A. Sample Pricing Framework

Service	Model	Typical Rate Range
Plea/Sentencing Consultation	Flat Fee	\$150–\$250 per case
Collateral Consequence Analysis	Flat Fee	\$150–\$300
Attorney Training Workshop	Hourly / Per Session	\$500–\$1,000 per presentation
Expert Report / Testimony	Hourly	\$150–\$250 per hour
Ongoing Attorney Retainer	Monthly Retainer	\$1,000–\$2,500 per month (varies by volume)

Rates may adjust by jurisdiction, experience level, and case complexity.

B. Payment Policies

- Always require a **written engagement agreement** signed by defense counsel.
- For new clients, request **partial payment upfront** (50%) and the remainder upon delivery.
- Accept electronic payments through secure methods (e.g., LawPay, Stripe, or Zelle for Business).
- Provide itemized invoices detailing deliverables.

C. Handling Non-Payment and Engagement Disputes

Payment disputes are an uncomfortable reality of any professional services practice. The best protection against them is a written engagement agreement signed before any work begins. The best resolution for them, when they occur, is a clear and documented process.

D. Pro-Bono Work and Sliding Scale Fees

The clients who most need sentencing consultation are frequently the ones who cannot afford it. Defendants represented by public defenders or court-appointed counsel are, by definition, individuals who have been found financially unable to retain private counsel. The gap between who needs this service and who can pay for it is a structural reality of indigent defense, and every sentencing consultant will be confronted with it.

How you navigate that gap is both a business decision and an ethical one. There is no single right answer. But having a clear policy before the question arises, rather than making it up case by case, protects your practice, ensures consistency, and allows you to serve the clients who need you most without undermining your financial sustainability.

Pro-Bono Work

Pro-bono consultation means providing your services at no charge. It is not charity, it is a professional commitment. Attorneys are expected by their bar associations to provide a certain amount of pro-bono legal service annually. Sentencing consultants who adopt a similar standard signal that they understand the mission of this work extends beyond the clients who can pay for it.

A workable approach is to designate a percentage of your annual caseload as pro-bono, typically five to ten percent. This creates a predictable commitment that you can plan around financially rather than an open-ended obligation that depletes your capacity. Public defender offices and legal aid organizations are the appropriate referral sources for pro-bono cases. Establish a relationship with one or two offices in your jurisdiction, make your pro-bono availability known, and let them refer cases to you within your designated capacity.

Document pro-bono work with the same rigor as paid work. The consultation summary, the comprehension acknowledgment, and the attorney file should look identical whether the client paid or not. Pro-bono does not mean informal, it means uncompensated. The professional standard does not change.

Sliding Scale Fees

A sliding scale fee structure adjusts your rate based on the client's ability to pay, typically within a defined range. For example, a consultant whose standard flat fee for a plea consultation is $250 might offer a sliding scale from $75 to $250 based on documented financial need. The attorney, not the client, typically communicates the financial circumstances and requests the adjusted rate.

To implement a sliding scale effectively:

- Set a floor below which you will not work, a minimum rate that covers your time and overhead without creating a loss. This is not the same as zero. Zero is pro-bono. A sliding scale floor is a reduced but still compensated rate.
- Require the request to come through the attorney in writing, with a brief description of the client's financial circumstances. This maintains the professional structure of the engagement and avoids placing the consultant in the position of adjudicating financial need directly with the client.

- Apply the sliding scale consistently, not selectively based on personal sympathy or the nature of the case. A written policy applied uniformly is a professional tool. An ad hoc adjustment made case by case creates the appearance of favoritism and makes your pricing unpredictable.
- Track reduced-fee and pro-bono work separately in your financial records. At year's end, review what percentage of your work was subsidized and whether that level is sustainable given your revenue from full-fee cases.

The Business Case for Serving Indigent Clients

Beyond the ethical argument, there is a practical one. Public defender offices handle the highest volume of criminal cases in any jurisdiction. A consultant who has established a track record of reliable, professional work with a public defender's office, even at reduced rates, will receive referrals from that office when they have clients who can pay. The relationship you build on a pro-bono case today is the referral that generates a full-fee case next month.

This is not a reason to undersell your services or treat reduced-fee work as a loss leader. It is a recognition that the legal community is smaller than it appears, that reputation travels through it quickly, and that a consultant who is known for doing good work regardless of the fee is a consultant who gets called.

Consulting Implication: Your pricing structure, including your pro-bono policy and your sliding scale range, should be documented in writing and available to any attorney who asks. Transparency about how you handle fee adjustments signals professionalism and prevents misunderstandings. Decide your policy before you are asked about it, put it in writing, and apply it consistently.

Prevention: What Your Engagement Agreement Must Include

- Scope of services, exactly what you will deliver, in what format, and by when.
- Fee structure, flat fee or hourly rate, total estimated cost, and the payment schedule.
- Deposit requirement, for new clients, requires 50 percent of the estimated fee before the first session. This is standard professional practice and protects you if the engagement is terminated early.
- Payment terms specify when invoices are due, typically net 14 or net 30, and any late payment fee.
- Dispute resolution, specify that any dispute will be resolved through mediation before litigation, and identify the governing jurisdiction.
- Termination clause: either party may terminate the engagement with written notice; fees for completed work are non-refundable.

Use a template engagement agreement reviewed by a business attorney in your state. Do not rely on verbal agreements for any engagement, regardless of how well you know the attorney.

When a Payment Dispute Arises

If an attorney disputes an invoice or fails to pay within the agreed terms, the response is professional and documented, not personal.

First, send a written notice by email confirming the outstanding balance, the original due date, and a request for payment within a specific additional timeframe, typically seven to fourteen days. Keep the tone neutral and factual.

Second, if the dispute involves a disagreement about what was delivered, refer to your engagement agreement and your consultation documentation. Your records are your evidence. If the work was completed as specified, the fee is owed.

Third, if payment is not received after a written notice, you have three options: negotiate a resolution directly, engage a collections professional, or, for amounts that justify the effort, pursue the claim in small claims court. Most jurisdictions allow claims up to $5,000–$10,000 in small claims without requiring an attorney.

What you should not do: continue providing services to an attorney who has an unresolved outstanding balance.

Consulting Implication: A signed engagement agreement is the single most important document in your business practice, more important than any consultation form. It sets expectations, protects your fees, and signals to every attorney you work with that you operate with the same professional discipline you bring to your consulting work. Make it a non-negotiable condition of every engagement from your first client forward.

Transparent billing builds credibility and reduces misunderstandings.

5. Marketing to Attorneys and Law Firms

A. Professional Networking

The most powerful marketing in this field is **relationship-based**. Focus on:

- Attending bar association events and continuing legal education (CLE) programs.

- Presenting short workshops for public defender offices and legal clinics.
- Joining professional organizations like the **National Association for Sentencing Reform** or the **American Correctional Association**.
- Maintaining an active LinkedIn presence, highlighting case law updates, success stories, and educational content.

B. Digital Presence

Create a clean, professional website that clearly communicates your services and credibility.

Key Website Sections:

1. **Home / Mission Statement:** concise and values-based.
2. **Services:** outline core offerings and deliverables.
3. **About:** include professional bio emphasizing expertise and transformation.
4. **Testimonials:** showcase feedback from attorneys and clients.
5. **Contact / Booking:** integrate a consultation request form.

Include professional headshots, certifications, and affiliations to signal trustworthiness.

C. Thought Leadership

Publish short articles or case analyses on topics such as:

- *"The Consultant's Role Under Frye and Lafler"*
- *"Mitigating Collateral Consequences Through Education"*
- *"The Hidden Sentence: Why Clients Deserve Full Information"*

Writing for bar journals or blogs establishes authority and visibility.

6. Referral and Retention Strategies

A. Building Attorney Referrals

Attorneys refer those they **trust**. Maintain trust through:

- Consistent communication.
- Meticulous documentation.
- On-time delivery.
- Confidentiality and discretion.

Follow up after each successful case with a professional thank-you note or email summarizing the collaboration's impact.

B. Retainer and Partnership Models

Offer flexible partnerships for firms handling multiple cases per month.

Example:

"For $1,500 per month, I provide up to 5 sentencing consultations, standardized forms, and written summaries for your office."

This model creates predictable revenue for you and predictable support for the attorney.

7. Scaling and Growth

Once your reputation is established, consider expansion through:

- **Hiring Associate Consultants:** Train others using your framework and templates.

- **Creating Online Courses:** Offer digital training for paralegals or law students.
- **Publishing Educational Materials:** Workbooks, checklists, or CLE guides (many of which you're already developing in this manual).
- **Collaborating with Advocacy Organizations:** Partner on community reentry programs or policy initiatives.

Long-Term Vision:

Your consulting business can evolve into a **sentencing education firm**, combining consulting, training, and advocacy to improve justice outcomes system-wide.

8. Branding and Professional Image

Your brand is not just a logo; it's your reputation in visual form.

The goal is *consistency* across all materials: business cards, website, presentations, and documents.

Branding Tips:

- Use clean, professional fonts (e.g., Lato, Montserrat, or Helvetica).
- Choose calming, trustworthy colors (blue, gray, or charcoal).
- Include a concise tagline that reflects mission and impact.

Sample Tagline Ideas:

- "Clarity in Sentencing. Integrity in Service."
- "Bridging Law and Life Through Informed Justice."
- "Helping Attorneys and Clients Make Informed Decisions."

9. Quality Control and Client Feedback

Establish a quality-assurance process that includes:

- Regular self-audits of documentation.
- Anonymous attorney feedback forms after each engagement.
- Post-consultation surveys for continuous improvement.

Sample Feedback Prompt:

"Did this consultation improve your client's understanding of their plea and sentence? Would you use this service again?"

Professional self-evaluation keeps your enterprise aligned with its mission and evolving legal standards.

10. Ethics and Business Integrity

Growth must never compromise ethics.
As your client base expands, maintain the same principles established earlier:

- Confidentiality
- Transparency
- Role boundaries
- Accountability

Never market your services with guarantees or emotional appeals. Instead, market **trust, structure, and results.**

Consulting Insight Box:

Your reputation is your marketing budget. Every satisfied attorney is a billboard you didn't have to pay for.

Case Study: Building a Sustainable Practice

Scenario:

A former corrections professional launches a sentencing consulting business after years of informal advising. Within one year, they secure ongoing contracts with two law firms, offer quarterly CLE workshops, and publish a white paper on plea comprehension.

Key to Success:

- Clear mission statement and documented methodology.
- Professional website and polished materials.
- Reliable, consistent delivery and communication with counsel.

By the second year, the consultant transitions from a one-person operation to a small firm, mentoring new consultants under the same ethical standards.

Conclusion: The Business of Purpose

Building a sentencing consulting business is not about chasing clients; it's about **creating credibility**.

Each consultation, report, and presentation strengthens your reputation as a professional who brings clarity to confusion and structure to chaos.

You are not selling information; you are offering **confidence** for attorneys, for clients, and for the justice system itself.

With a strong mission, ethical structure, and disciplined business model, your consulting practice becomes more than a service. It becomes a platform for reform, proof that integrity and professionalism can transform even the most complex corners of the criminal justice process.

Key Takeaways

- Your mission and value proposition define your niche and purpose.
- Treat consulting as a professional enterprise: contracts, structure, insurance, and documentation.
- Relationship-based marketing and attorney referrals drive growth.
- Scale through training, publishing, and partnerships, not shortcuts.
- Ethics remains your greatest competitive advantage.

Chapter 15: Training and Thought Leadership

Introduction: From Service to Influence

The most powerful consultants don't just inform clients, they *educate systems.* By sharing your expertise with attorneys, law students, and justice professionals, you transform individual case work into institutional progress.

Training and thought leadership elevate your work from one-on-one consultation to field-wide change. Through continuing legal education (CLEs), workshops, and public speaking, you help shape a culture of justice that values informed consent, ethical defense, and human understanding.

This chapter provides the roadmap to becoming a recognized authority, not just a consultant, but a *teacher of justice.*

1. The Role of the Sentencing Consultant as Educator

Every attorney who hears your presentation and every student who attends your seminar carries your message forward.

Education amplifies impact.

Your expertise covers four essential learning domains:

1. **Sentencing Law and Practice:** grounding in case law (*Frye*, *Lafler*, *Padilla*, *Strickland*).
2. **Client Communication:** trauma-informed and comprehension-focused methods.
3. **Correctional Realities:** explaining how time, placement, and classification actually work.
4. **Ethical Practice:** ensuring that client rights are not only protected, but understood.

When you teach these concepts, you're not just transferring knowledge; you're cultivating competence, compassion, and accountability across the legal system.

2. Designing Professional Training

Training others requires both **expert content** and **intentional design**. Whether teaching attorneys, paralegals, or students, your sessions should follow a structured educational flow:

A. The Four-Part Learning Model

1. **Foundation:** Explain the constitutional and ethical framework (why it matters).
2. **Application:** Walk through real examples (how it works).
3. **Practice:** Engage participants through exercises or roleplay (how it feels).
4. **Reflection:** Encourage personal insight and professional adaptation (how it changes practice).

B. Common Training Formats

- **CLE Seminars (1–3 hours):** Focused, practical legal education.
- **Workshops (Half- or Full-Day):** Interactive exercises, case scenarios, group analysis.
- **University Guest Lectures:** Contextual storytelling that links theory to practice.
- **Keynote Addresses:** Motivational, mission-driven presentations for conferences.

Each format has its own rhythm, but all must be rooted in truth, clarity, and engagement.

3. Developing CLE and Workshop Content

A. Core Curriculum Topics

You can build multiple trainings around your existing manual's framework:

Training Title	Focus Area	Target Audience
Understanding the Duty to Inform: Frye, Lafler, and Padilla in Practice	Constitutional law & effective counsel	Defense attorneys, public defenders
Bridging Law and Life: Communicating Sentencing to Clients	Comprehension & trauma-informed communication	Paralegals, social workers, consultants

Training Title	Focus Area	Target Audience
The Hidden Sentence: Collateral Consequences and Ethical Disclosure	Ethical and systemic impacts	CLEs, advocacy groups
The Consultant's Role in Modern Defense Strategy	Defense collaboration and documentation	Law firms, mitigation specialists
From Prison to Professional: Reimagining Lived Experience as Expertise	Lived experience and reentry education	Universities, criminal justice programs

B. Learning Objectives

Each session should include 3–5 measurable outcomes. For example:

- Participants will be able to explain the holding in *Lafler v. Cooper.*
- Participants will identify three collateral consequences of felony convictions.
- Participants will demonstrate the teach-back method during roleplay exercises.

Clear objectives ensure accreditation approval for CLE or continuing education programs.

4. Structuring an Engaging Presentation

A. The "Story–Structure–Strategy" Method

Start with a Story:

Open with a compelling narrative, a real experience that illustrates the stakes of misunderstanding in sentencing.

Example: "I once met a man who thought he was serving eight years when he'd actually agreed to fourteen."

Build the Structure:

Transition to the legal and procedural framework that explains how that misunderstanding happens.

Deliver the Strategy:

End with clear, actionable steps attorneys can take to prevent it.

This approach keeps professionals engaged while grounding your expertise in authenticity and law.

B. Visuals and Aids

- Use PowerPoint or Canva to create clean slides with minimal text.
- Integrate quotes from Supreme Court cases and ethical codes.
- Include charts, sentencing timelines, or flow diagrams for clarity.
- End with a QR code linking to downloadable materials (handouts, checklists, or this manual).

Pro Tip:

Keep slides visual, not verbal. The story comes from you, not the screen.

5. Building a Thought Leadership Brand

A. Establishing Your Voice

Thought leadership grows from consistent visibility and credibility.

Your writing and speaking should consistently reflect three themes:

1. **Integrity:** grounded in law and ethics.
2. **Humanity:** centered on clients' lived experiences.
3. **Transformation:** focused on progress, not blame.

These pillars make your message distinct and trusted across audiences.

B. Publishing for Credibility

Write and publish short, authoritative articles such as:

- *"Bridging the Gap Between Counsel and Client Understanding"*
- *"The Real-World Impact of Missouri v. Frye on Defense Practice"*
- *"Why Collateral Consequences Are a Constitutional Concern"*

Submit to:

- State Bar Association newsletters.
- The National Association of Criminal Defense Lawyers (NACDL).
- Correctional and reentry publications.

- University criminal justice journals.

Writing builds intellectual credibility; speaking amplifies it.

6. Becoming a Public Speaker

A. Speaking Opportunities

Look for engagements at:

- State and regional bar associations.
- Legal aid and public defender conferences.
- University criminal justice programs.
- Reentry or policy advocacy summits.
- Correctional education conferences.

These audiences value expertise that blends **lived experience** with **professional insight**, your unique strength.

B. Speaker Profile Essentials

Include on your website or media kit:

- Professional bio (150–200 words).
- Headshot and title (e.g., *David R. Carrillo, MBA – Sentencing Consultant & Educator*).
- Keynote topics and CLE titles.
- Contact and booking information.
- Testimonials from previous hosts or attendees.

C. Sample Keynote Outline: "From Life Without Parole to Educator and Consultant"

- **Opening Narrative:** Your journey from incarceration to education.
- **System Insight:** How misunderstanding plea deals shapes outcomes.
- **Transformation:** How knowledge and purpose create new paths.
- **Action Steps:** How attorneys and institutions can build understanding into practice.

Authenticity makes the keynote memorable; professionalism makes it repeatable.

7. Partnering with Institutions

Strategic partnerships create recurring opportunities and stability.

Potential Partners:

- **Law Schools:** Guest lectures, adjunct roles, and curriculum development.
- **Bar Associations:** Accredited CLE provider relationships.
- **State Agencies:** Public Defenders, other Alternate Defense Counsel programs
- **Nonprofits:** Co-facilitation of reentry education or community legal literacy.
- **Universities and Correctional Education Programs:** Instructor roles or curriculum advisory panels.

Develop memoranda of understanding (MOUs) that outline scope, deliverables, and compensation for recurring engagements.

8. Monetizing Educational Content

Your expertise can become a self-sustaining revenue stream through:

- **Online Courses:** Host via Teachable, Thinkific, or Udemy (e.g., "The Consultant's Guide to Sentencing Practice").
- **Webinars:** Offer 60–90-minute sessions with Q&A.
- **Resource Packages:** Sell editable templates, checklists, and intake forms.
- **Books and Workbooks:** Publish manuals like this one as companion educational tools.
- **Certification Programs:** Train and certify future consultants under your methodology.

Education not only multiplies your income; it multiplies your influence.

9. Ethics in Public Education

Even in public forums, ethics apply:

- Do not reveal client names or case details.
- Always credit sources and collaborators.
- Avoid offering individualized legal advice during workshops.
- Maintain balance between advocacy and neutrality; your credibility depends on both.
- Professional educators teach truth with discretion.

10. Sustaining Thought Leadership

Becoming a leader requires consistency more than charisma. Develop a long-term system for visibility and credibility:

Quarterly Thought Leadership Plan

Month	Activity
January–March	Write and publish one article or blog post.
April–June	Deliver one CLE or workshop presentation.
July–September	Guest lecture or record a podcast interview.
October–December	Update materials and reflect on growth goals.

Every quarter, your voice strengthens. Every year, your influence grows.

Case Study: From Consultant to Educator

Scenario:

A sentencing consultant begins offering small CLE presentations at local bar associations. Within two years, demand expands across multiple states. The consultant publishes an eBook on plea comprehension, launches an online course, and partners with a state university to co-teach a course on sentencing ethics.

Outcome:

The consultant transitions from case-by-case work to national influence, shaping how defense attorneys, policymakers, and educators approach sentencing communication.

Conclusion: Leadership Through Education

Thought leadership is the evolution of service. You began as a bridge between attorneys and clients; now, you become a bridge between disciplines, guiding the legal profession toward greater clarity, compassion, and competence.

By teaching others what you have lived, learned, and structured, you transform your work into a legacy; one that continues to educate, empower, and reform long after the courtroom lights fade.

Your voice, your framework, and your integrity are the curriculum the system needs.

Key Takeaways

- Education extends your influence beyond individual cases.
- Use structured design for CLEs, workshops, and lectures.
- Blend narrative authenticity with professional expertise.
- Thought leadership requires consistency and ethical grounding.
- Influence grows through clarity, credibility, and compassion.

Epilogue: Purpose as Profession

What You Now Carry

The Preface of this manual opened with a simple observation: defendants make the most consequential decisions of their lives without truly understanding what those decisions mean. They hear the words, but not the weight. They see the years, but not the realities.

You have now spent fifteen chapters learning how to change that.

You understand the constitutional framework that makes this work not just useful but necessary. You understand the three pathways a sentence can take and what each one means in a person's life. You know how to conduct a consultation, how to document it, how to work alongside an attorney without overstepping, and how to explain a release mechanism to a client who has never thought about earned time in their life. You know when to refer, how to adapt, and why the record built inside a correctional facility is as important as the plea entered before the gavel falls.

That knowledge is not abstract. It is the difference between a client who walks into a plea hearing informed and one who walks out of prison years later asking why no one told them what they agreed to.

The Profession You Are Entering

Sentencing consultation is not yet a household term. There is no licensing board, no formal certification, no established career path that leads a person to this work. What exists instead is a gap, a real, documented, constitutionally significant gap between what attorneys are required to communicate and what clients actually comprehend, and a growing number of people who understand both the gap and how to fill it.

You are now among them.

That carries weight. The clients who will sit across from you are not abstractions. They are people facing the most disorienting moment of their lives, trying to make a decision whose consequences will unfold over years they cannot yet imagine. They will not always be easy to reach. They will not always trust you immediately. They will sometimes be frightened in ways they cannot name and resistant in ways they cannot explain. And they will carry whatever understanding, or misunderstanding, leaves that consultation room with them for the duration of their sentence.

This manual has given you the tools. The work itself requires something the manual cannot give you: the willingness to sit with a person in that moment, to speak clearly about hard things, and to believe that understanding, even in the worst circumstances, is worth the effort of creating it.

The Standard You Set

Every time a client can restate the terms of their plea in their own words, you have done your job. Every time a family understands why they cannot visit for the first six weeks of intake, they are spared a confusion that compounds grief. Every time an attorney has a documented record showing that their client was genuinely informed, not merely present, the integrity of that proceeding is protected.

These are not dramatic outcomes. They do not generate headlines. But they are the outcomes that matter most to the people living inside them, and they accumulate into something larger than any single case: a standard of practice that did not exist before, being built one consultation at a time by practitioners who understood that justice requires more than representation.

The Foreword to this manual notes that attorneys are asked to be counselors, social workers, therapists, and financial advisors in addition to advocates, and that they cannot do all of it alone. The sentencing consultant exists to take one piece of that burden and carry it with the rigor it deserves. When you do that work well, you are not supplementing representation. You are completing it.

A Note on Where This Began

This manual was written by someone who spent thirty-one years inside the system it describes. Not studying it from the outside. Inside it, in segregation cells, on general population yards, in classrooms built from nothing, in a clemency interview on a Zoom call from a case manager's office on December 22, 2023.

Every chapter in this book draws on that experience, even when the text does not say so directly. The observation that the first ninety days of a sentence shape everything that follows is not a research finding. It is something lived. The argument that a client who understands their release mechanism before they enter the system is fundamentally different from one who discovers it after their first violation is not theoretical. It is the difference between purposeful navigation and bewildered survival.

That experience does not make this manual the final word on sentencing consultation. It makes it a beginning, a foundation built from something real, offered to practitioners who will take it further than any single author can.

What Comes Next

This field will grow. The cases that define the duty to inform, Strickland, Frye, Lafler, and Padilla, were decided decades apart, each one extending the constitutional obligation one step further toward genuine comprehension. The trajectory points in one direction. Courts, bar associations, and defense organizations are slowly recognizing that informed consent in a plea proceeding requires more than a form signed in a courthouse hallway.

The practitioners who enter this field now are not following an established path. They are making one. Every documented consultation, every attorney relationship built on demonstrated competence, every client who walks into a sentence understanding what they agreed to, all of it becomes precedent for what this profession can be.

You are not too late for this work. You are early. And the standard you hold yourself to now will shape what the field becomes for the practitioners who come after you.

Justice is not complete until it's understood.

Go make sure it is.

David R. Carrillo, MBA
Founder, David R. Carrillo Consulting, LLC

Appendix A—Core Legal Foundations

The following cases and ethical standards form the constitutional and professional basis for sentencing consultation. Each entry identifies the holding and its direct relevance to the consultant's role.

Case Law

1. Strickland v. Washington, 466 U.S. 668 (1984)

Holding: Established the two-prong test for ineffective assistance of counsel. To prevail, a defendant must show (1) that counsel's performance fell below an objective standard of reasonableness, and (2) that the deficient performance prejudiced the defense, meaning there is a reasonable probability the outcome would have been different but for counsel's errors.

Consulting Relevance: Strickland sets the constitutional floor for all attorney conduct in criminal proceedings, including plea negotiations. Sentencing consultants support defense attorneys in meeting this standard by improving client comprehension, ensuring informed consent is genuine rather than formal, and creating a documented record of the communication that occurred.

2. Hill v. Lockhart, 474 U.S. 52 (1985)

Holding: Extended the Strickland two-prong test directly to the plea-bargaining context. A defendant who accepts a plea based on counsel's inaccurate advice about sentencing consequences may have a viable constitutional claim. The prejudice prong requires showing a reasonable probability that, but for counsel's errors, the defendant would not have pleaded guilty.

Consulting Relevance: Hill is the case that makes the sentencing consultant's work legally significant at its most foundational level. Inaccurate advice about parole eligibility, sentence length, or conditions of confinement, precisely the kind of misunderstanding consultants prevent, can constitute ineffective assistance under Hill. Consultants who accurately explain these consequences and document the explanation directly support this standard.

3. Missouri v. Frye, 566 U.S. 134 (2012)

Holding: Defense counsel has the duty to communicate formal plea offers from the prosecution to the accused. Failure to convey a plea offer before it expires can constitute ineffective assistance under Strickland.

Consulting Relevance: Consultants support the Frye duty by ensuring that plea offers, once communicated, are genuinely understood. When a client cannot restate the terms of an offer in their own words, communication has not been completed. Consultant documentation of comprehension, signed acknowledgment forms, consultation summaries, creates evidence that the communication standard was met.

4. Lafler v. Cooper, 566 U.S. 156 (2012)

Holding: Deficient legal advice that causes a defendant to reject a favorable plea offer and receive a harsher sentence after trial can constitute ineffective assistance under the Sixth Amendment. The prejudice analysis asks whether the defendant would have accepted the plea but for counsel's errors.

Consulting Relevance: Lafler addresses the cost of misinformation. Consultants prevent Lafler scenarios by providing objective, accurate explanations of sentencing exposure under both plea and trial outcomes, correcting misunderstandings about likely consequences, and documenting that the client understood the realistic options before deciding.

5. Padilla v. Kentucky, 559 U.S. 356 (2010)

Holding: Failure to advise a client about the immigration consequences of a guilty plea constitutes ineffective assistance of counsel under the Sixth Amendment. When deportation is a clear consequence of the conviction, counsel must advise the client accordingly.

Consulting Relevance: Padilla extended the duty to inform beyond direct sentencing consequences to collateral consequences that flow from conviction. Consultants assist attorneys in identifying and disclosing the full landscape of collateral consequences, immigration status, employment restrictions, housing eligibility, civil rights, and more. For non-citizen clients, flagging potential immigration exposure to the attorney is a mandatory step in every consultation.

Ethical and Professional Standards

ABA Standards for Criminal Justice: Defense Function (4th Edition)

§ 4-5.1 — **Advising the Client:** Counsel has a duty to keep clients informed about the status of the case and to explain matters sufficiently to permit the client to make informed decisions.

§ 4-6.1 — **Plea Discussions:** Defense counsel should promptly communicate and explain to the accused all plea offers made by the prosecutor. Counsel should ensure the client understands the terms and consequences of any plea offer.

§ 4-8.2 — **Client Communication:** Counsel has a duty to advise the client with candor about the realities of the case, including potential penalties, likely outcomes, and the consequences of accepting or rejecting a plea.

State Rules of Professional Conduct—Communication

Most state rules of professional conduct include a communication rule requiring attorneys to keep clients reasonably informed and to explain matters sufficiently for clients to make informed decisions. Consultants operating under attorney direction should be familiar with the rule in their jurisdiction. Reference your state bar's Rules of Professional Conduct, typically Rule 1.4 or its equivalent.

Unauthorized Practice of Law—Consultant Boundaries

Sentencing consultants are not licensed attorneys and must not provide legal advice, represent clients before tribunals, or perform functions reserved for licensed counsel. All consultation activity should be conducted under the direction and supervision of defense counsel. Consultants explain, translate, and document — they do not advise on legal strategy or speak for the client in any legal proceeding.

Appendix B—Consultation Templates and Forms

Each form in this appendix may be reproduced for professional use with attribution to David R. Carrillo Consulting, LLC. These documents are designed to support the consultation process, document client comprehension, and create a professional record for the attorney's file. They are educational tools, not legal documents, and should be reviewed by the supervising attorney before use in any jurisdiction.

Form 1—Client Intake and Case Summary

Purpose: Establish the foundational facts of the case, assess the client's baseline comprehension, and identify consultation priorities before the first substantive session.

Case Information

Client Name: ______________________________________

Date: ______________________

Case Number: _________________________________

Court / Jurisdiction: _______________________________

Defense Counsel: _________________________________

Firm / Office: _______________________________

Charge(s):

____

Plea Offered: _________________________________

Offer Expiration: ___________________________

Client Background

Primary Language: ______________________________

Interpreter Required? _______ **Yes / No** _

Highest Education Level:

____

Prior Criminal History:

____

Prior Incarceration? _______ **Yes / No** _

If yes, state/system: _________________________________

Initial Comprehension Assessment

Ask the client to describe, in their own words, their understanding of each item. Note the response — do not coach.

What are you charged with?

____

What does the plea offer require you to agree to?

____

What happens if you reject the plea and go to trial?

____

What does the sentence mean for your daily life?

____

Comprehension Rating (Consultant Assessment)

☐ Strong — client can restate all key terms accurately without prompting

☐ Partial — client understands the charge but not the full consequences

☐ Minimal — client understands little beyond the sentence number

☐ Requires adapted approach — note language, cognitive, or other factors below

Consultant Notes:

____

____

Consultation Priorities Identified

☐ Sentence length and what it means in practice

☐ Release mechanism (parole eligibility / earned time / federal)

☐ Conditions of confinement and classification

☐ Collateral consequences

☐ Family impact and contact during incarceration

☐ Reentry considerations

☐ Other:

Signatures

Client Signature: ______________________ **Date:** ____________

Consultant Signature: ______________________ **Date:** ____________

Form 2 — Plea Understanding Acknowledgment

Purpose: Document that the client has been advised of and understands the material terms and consequences of the plea offer. This form should be signed before plea entry and retained in the attorney's file.

Client and Case Information

Client Name: ____

Date: ______________________

Case Number: ______________________________________

Consulting Date(s): ______________________________

Defense Counsel:

____

Acknowledgment of Understanding

I, __________________________________, acknowledge that a sentencing consultant retained by my defense counsel has reviewed the following matters with me. I have had an opportunity to ask questions and have received explanations in language I understand.

I understand each of the following:

☐ The nature of the charges I am pleading to and what conduct those charges describe.

☐ The sentencing range available to the judge under the plea offer, including any mandatory minimum terms.

☐ The specific terms of the plea offer: length of incarceration, probation or supervised release, and any conditions attached.

☐ My right to a jury trial and that by pleading guilty I waive that right.

☐ That the judge is not bound by the plea agreement and may impose a sentence within the statutory range.

☐ The release mechanism that governs my sentence — including parole eligibility, earned time, or good time — and how my conduct will affect it.

☐ The likely conditions of incarceration, including the intake process and classification system.

I have been advised of the following collateral consequences that may apply to my conviction:

☐ Employment: restrictions on occupational licenses, professional certifications, or certain categories of employment.

☐ Housing: potential ineligibility for public housing or Section 8 assistance.

☐ Education: possible effects on financial aid or campus housing eligibility.

☐ Immigration: potential deportation, inadmissibility, or effects on citizenship (if applicable).

☐ Family: potential effects on custody, visitation, or parental rights.

☐ Civil rights: loss of voting rights, firearm rights, or eligibility for jury service.

☐ Financial: restitution obligations, fines, fees, and loss of public benefits.

☐ I am making this decision voluntarily, without coercion, and with a genuine understanding of its consequences.

☐ I have been given the opportunity to ask questions and all questions have been answered to my satisfaction.

Signatures

Client Signature: ______________________ **Date:** ______________

Consultant Signature: ______________________ **Date:** ______________

Attorney Signature (Witness): ______________________ **Date:** ______________

This form should be retained in the attorney's case file. A copy should be provided to the client upon request.

Form 3—Collateral Consequence Review Worksheet

Purpose: Systematically identify collateral consequences relevant to this client's conviction. Check all that apply, note the specific consequence, and flag any area requiring referral to a specialist.

Client Name: ______________________________
Date: ______________
Conviction / Charge:
____

	Category	Specific Consequences to Review	Notes / Details	Refer?

☐	**Employment**	Loss of occupational license; bar from government employment; background check barriers; restrictions on working with vulnerable populations.		Yes / No
☐	**Housing**	Ineligibility for public housing (HUD); denial of Section 8 vouchers; private landlord background check barriers; sex offender registry housing restrictions.		Yes / No
☐	**Education**	Loss of federal financial aid eligibility (drug offenses); denial of campus housing; disclosure requirements on applications.		Yes / No
☐	**Immigration**	Deportation/removal; inadmissibility; denial of naturalization; loss of lawful permanent resident status; visa ineligibility.		Yes / No
☐	**Family & Parental**	Termination of parental rights proceedings; supervised visitation only; restrictions on adoption eligibility; effects on custody arrangements.		Yes / No

☐	**Civil Rights**	Loss of voting rights (varies by state); prohibition on firearm possession; ineligibility for jury service; restrictions on public office.		Yes / No
☐	**Financial**	Restitution obligations; court fines and fees; loss of Social Security benefits; loss of SNAP / TANF eligibility; tax consequences.		Yes / No
☐	**Registration**	Sex offender registry; violent offender registry; drug offender notification requirements; duration and conditions of registration.		Yes / No
☐	**Professional Licensing**	Bar from licensed professions (law, medicine, teaching, contracting, etc.); revocation of existing licenses.		Yes / No
☐	**Military / Veterans**	Ineligibility for military service; loss of or effects on VA benefits; effects on security clearance.		Yes / No

Consultant Notes / Additional Consequences Identified:

____

____

Referrals Made (immigration attorney, benefits specialist, etc.):

____

Consultant Signature: ____________________________ **Date:** __________________

Form 4 — Consultation Summary Report (Attorney Version)

Purpose: Provide defense counsel with a written summary of the consultation for inclusion in the case file. This report documents what was covered, the client's demonstrated level of comprehension, and any recommended follow-up actions.

Case and Consultation Information

Client Name: ______________________________

Date of Report: ________________

Case Number: __________________________

Consulting Date(s): ______________________

Defense Counsel: ___________________________

Consultant: ________________________

Number of Sessions: ________________

Total Time: ________________

Matters Reviewed

- ☐ Charge elements and what the plea admits to
- ☐ Sentencing range and plea terms
- ☐ Release mechanism (parole / earned time / federal credits)
- ☐ Conditions of confinement and classification process
- ☐ Collateral consequences — see Form 3 attached
- ☐ Family impact and incarceration contact
- ☐ Reentry considerations
- ☐ Other:

Client Comprehension Assessment

Overall comprehension level:

- ☐ Strong — client demonstrated accurate understanding of all material terms
- ☐ Adequate — client understood key terms with some gaps identified and addressed
- ☐ Partial — significant comprehension gaps remain; follow-up recommended
- ☐ Concerns noted — see below

Summary of comprehension gaps or concerns:

____

____

Recommended Follow-Up Actions for Counsel

1.

____

____

2.

____

____

3.

____

____

Attachments

- ☐ Form 1 — Client Intake and Case Summary
- ☐ Form 2 — Plea Understanding Acknowledgment
- ☐ Form 3 — Collateral Consequence Review Worksheet
- ☐ Interpreter certification/qualifications (if applicable)
- ☐ Other:

Confidentiality Notice

This report and all attached forms are confidential. They were prepared at the request of defense counsel and are protected under the attorney-client privilege to the extent applicable in this jurisdiction. The consultant shall not disclose or discuss the contents of this report with any party other than defense counsel without express written authorization.

Consultant Signature: ______________________________ **Date:** ____________________

Appendix C — Professional Tools for Consultants

The following tools are designed for ongoing use in the consultant's practice. They are not client-facing documents but internal reference materials for maintaining professional standards, consistency, and ethical conduct.

Pre-Consultation Checklist

Complete before each consultation session. Check each item before meeting with the client.

Case Preparation

☐ Obtain and review the charging document and applicable statutory sentencing range.

☐ Review the plea offer in full, including all conditions and attached obligations.

☐ Identify the applicable release mechanism: parole-eligible, determinate/earned time, or federal.

☐ Calculate the estimated release date under maximum earned/good time credits.

☐ Identify applicable collateral consequence categories for this offense and client profile.

☐ Confirm whether the client is a non-citizen—if yes, flag immigration counsel to the attorney immediately.

☐ Confirm whether a professional interpreter is needed and arrange one if so.

☐ Review any prior consultation notes or case documents.

Logistics

☐ Confirm consultation location, time, and access arrangements with the attorney.

☐ Confirm that forms (Forms 1–4) are prepared and ready.

☐ Confirm that all prior signed documents from this client are securely stored.

Post-Consultation

☐ Teach-back completed—client restated key terms in their own words.

☐ All applicable forms signed and copies provided to the attorney.

☐ Consultation Summary Report (Form 4) completed and transmitted to the attorney.

☐ Any referrals made are documented in Form 3 and noted in Form 4.

☐ All documents stored under the retention protocol below.

The Carrillo Consultation Sequence—Session Reference Card

The following one-page version is designed for printing as a single card for consultants to keep on hand during sessions, for distribution in CLE packets, and for inclusion in Appendix C alongside the other professional tools. It condenses each step to its essential action items.

THE CARRILLO CONSULTATION SEQUENCE *Six Steps — Every Consultation — Every Pathway*	
1	**Identify the Pathway**

	Which of the Three Pathways? | Name it. | Explain what it means in plain terms. | Correct the most common misconception for this pathway.
2	**Map the Authority Structure** Who controls daily life? | What can that authority do? | What does a violation look like in this pathway?
3	**Explain Daily Reality** Intake process and contact restrictions. | Classification — level, what drives it, what it means. | Conditions: facility/placement/supervision.
	Explain Failure Consequences Name the violation consequence — in days, not vague warnings. | Connect it to the release date. | Make it real, not hypothetical.
5	**Explain the Release Mechanism** Which system: parole/formula/federal? | Calculate: best case, realistic, worst case. | Address post-release supervision.
6	**Confirm Comprehension—Teach-Back** "Tell me the pathway and what it means." | "When do you come home, and what determines it?" | "What does a serious write-up cost you?" | No signatures until all three confirmed.

Ethical Decision Framework

When a situation arises that is uncertain or outside routine practice, work through the following questions in order before acting.

Question	If the answer is no or uncertain —

Is this action within my role as a sentencing consultant, not legal counsel?	Stop. Refer the matter to defense counsel. Do not proceed.
Have I received direction or authorization from the supervising attorney?	Pause. Clarify scope with counsel before proceeding.
Could this action compromise the client's confidentiality or attorney-client privilege?	Document but do not disclose externally. Consult the attorney.
Have I verified the client's comprehension through teach-back, not just acknowledgment?	Continue the session. Do not obtain signatures until comprehension is confirmed.
Am I staying within my documented areas of expertise?	Acknowledge the limit. Make the appropriate referral. Document both.
Would I be comfortable if this action appeared in the attorney's case file?	Reconsider. Consult the attorney if uncertain.

Documentation Retention Policy

All client documents, signed forms, consultation notes, and correspondence must be retained in accordance with the following minimum standards. Consultants should also verify any applicable jurisdictional requirements.

- Retain all client forms, consultation summaries, and signed documents for a minimum of five years from the date of the last consultation, or longer if required by the supervising attorney's jurisdiction.

- Store all physical documents in a locked filing system accessible only to the consultant and authorized staff.
- Store all digital records in encrypted, password-protected systems. Do not use personal email or consumer cloud storage for client documents.
- Do not retain unnecessary personal identifiers beyond the purpose of the consultation. When documents are no longer required, dispose of physical copies by shredding and digital copies by secure deletion.
- In the event of a subpoena or legal process directed at consultation records, notify the supervising attorney immediately before responding.

Referral Directory Template

Maintain a current list of specialists for referral across the following categories. Update annually or whenever a referral source changes.

Specialist Type	Name / Organization	Contact	Notes
Immigration Attorney			
Mental Health Mitigation Specialist			
Veterans Treatment Court Coordinator			
VA-Accredited Benefits Agent			

Forensic Psychologist			
Interpreter Service			
Juvenile Defense Specialist			
Reentry Case Manager			

Appendix D—Sample CLE Outline

Program Title	**Understanding the Duty to Inform: Sentencing Consultation and the Constitutional Standard**
Duration	90 minutes (1.5 CLE credit hours, including 0.5 ethics)
Format	Lecture with interactive case scenario and Q&A
Presenter	David R. Carrillo, MBA — Sentencing Consultant, David R. Carrillo Consulting, LLC
Audience	Criminal defense attorneys, public defenders, law students

Learning Objectives

Upon completion of this program, participants will be able to:

1. Identify the constitutional basis for the duty to inform clients about plea terms and sentencing consequences, with reference to Strickland, Hill, Frye, Lafler, and Padilla.
2. Explain the role and scope of a sentencing consultant and how that role supports, without replacing, the attorney-client relationship.
3. Apply a consultation framework to ensure genuine client comprehension before plea entry, including teach-back verification and documentation.
4. Identify the categories of collateral consequences that must be addressed under Padilla and its progeny.
5. Recognize when a case involves a special population, youth, mental health, substance use, non-English-speaking, or veteran clients, and identify the appropriate specialist referral.

Program Agenda

Time	Topic	Format
0:00	Opening: Why informed consent in plea bargaining matters — the gap between what attorneys are required to do and what clients actually comprehend.	Lecture
0:10	Constitutional framework: Strickland, Hill, Frye, Lafler, and Padilla — what each case requires and how they combine to define the duty to inform.	Lecture
0:25	The sentencing consultant's role: what it includes, what it excludes, and how it supports the attorney without creating liability.	Lecture
0:35	The consultation in practice: the five-phase process, teach-back verification, and documentation that protects the attorney and the client.	Lecture + Q&A
0:50	Interactive case scenario: a client accepts a plea without understanding the release mechanism. Participants work through what went wrong and how to prevent it.	Group Exercise
1:10	Ethics segment: confidentiality, UPL boundaries, and the limits of the consultant's role — with reference to ABA Standards §§ 4-5.1, 4-6.1, and 4-8.2.	Lecture

1:20	Q&A and closing: how to engage a sentencing consultant, what to expect from the relationship, and available resources.	Discussion

Materials Provided to Participants

- Program outline (this document)
- Case law summary—Appendix A of Inside the Sentence
- Form 2—Plea Understanding Acknowledgment (sample)
- Form 3—Collateral Consequence Review Worksheet (sample)
- Consultant referral and engagement information
- Certificate of completion

Accreditation Note

This program is designed for submission to state bar CLE accreditation bodies. The ethics segment addresses competence (ABA Model Rule 1.1), communication (Rule 1.4), and confidentiality (Rule 1.6) in the context of consulting relationships. Presenters seeking accreditation should submit the program outline, learning objectives, and speaker biography to the relevant state authority at least 60 days before delivery.

Appendix E—Resources and Recommended Reading

The following resources are recommended for sentencing consultants building their knowledge base, staying current with legal developments, and connecting with professional communities. This list is not exhaustive and should be updated as the field evolves.

Professional Organizations

National Association of Criminal Defense Lawyers (NACDL)

nacdl.org — The primary professional organization for criminal defense attorneys. Publishes The Champion magazine, maintains a resource library on plea practice, sentencing, and collateral consequences, and offers training programs relevant to consultant development.

American Bar Association—Criminal Justice Section

americanbar.org/groups/criminal justice—Publishes the ABA Standards for Criminal Justice: Defense Function, a foundational reference for sentencing consultants. Provides access to ethics opinions, CLE programming, and criminal justice policy resources.

National Legal Aid & Defender Association (NLADA)

nlada.org — Represents public defenders and civil legal aid attorneys. A valuable resource for consultants working primarily with public defender offices, including guidance on standards for indigent defense.

The Sentencing Project

sentencingproject.org—Leading research and advocacy organization on sentencing policy, mass incarceration, and racial disparities. Publishes accessible summaries of sentencing trends, state-by-state data, and research on the collateral consequences of conviction.

Vera Institute of Justice

vera.org—Research and policy organization with extensive work on prison reform, correctional education, reentry, and the human costs of incarceration. Particularly useful for consultants developing expertise in Chapters 14 and 15 subject matter.

Legal Reference and Case Law

ABA Standards for Criminal Justice: Defense Function, 4th Edition

The authoritative professional standard for defense attorney conduct. Sections 4-5.1 (Advising the Client), 4-6.1 (Plea Discussions), and 4-8.2 (Client Communication) are directly relevant to sentencing consultation practice. Available through the ABA.

Collateral Consequences of Criminal Convictions: Law, Policy, and Practice—Margaret Love, Jenny Roberts & Cecelia Klingele

The most comprehensive practitioner guide to collateral consequences, organized by category and jurisdiction. An essential desk reference for any consultant working through the disclosure requirements addressed in Chapter 5.

Understanding Criminal Procedure—Joshua Dressler & Alan Michaels

A leading academic text on criminal procedure, including plea bargaining, sentencing, and post-conviction proceedings. Useful background reading for consultants seeking a deeper understanding of the constitutional framework.

Robina Institute of Criminal Law and Criminal Justice—Profiles in Parole Release and Revocation

robinainstitute.umn.edu—State-by-state profiles of parole release systems, sentencing structures, and good time and earned time laws. An essential reference for consultants working across multiple jurisdictions.

Government and Policy Resources

Bureau of Justice Statistics (BJS)

bjs.ojp.gov—The federal statistical agency for justice data. Publishes the Prisoners series, the Survey of Prison Inmates, and data on plea bargaining trends. Primary source for incarceration statistics cited in practice and advocacy.

National Institute of Corrections (NIC)

nicic.gov — Federal agency providing training, technical assistance, and research to state and local correctional agencies. Maintains a library of resources on classification systems, risk assessment, and programming that directly inform Chapters 14 and 15.

Prison Policy Initiative

prisonpolicy.org—Research organization producing accessible data and analysis on parole systems, incarceration rates, and state-by-state sentencing comparisons. The 2024 Parole in Perspective series is particularly relevant for consultants explaining release mechanisms to clients.

Collateral Consequences Resource Center

ccresourcecenter.org—A comprehensive database of state and federal laws imposing collateral consequences of conviction, organized by offense and consequence type. An essential research tool for the disclosure work addressed in Chapter 5.

Correctional Education and Reentry

RAND Corporation—Correctional Education Studies

rand.org—RAND's landmark research on the effectiveness of correctional education demonstrates that participation in educational programs reduces recidivism and improves employment outcomes. Foundational support for the arguments made in Chapter 15.

Adams State University—Prison Education Program

adams.edu—Adams State University operates one of the nation's prison education programs, offering degree programs inside Colorado correctional facilities. A model for correctional higher education partnerships nationwide.

Second Chance Pell Program—U.S. Department of Education

ed.gov—Information on Pell Grant eligibility for incarcerated students restored under the Second Chance Pell program. Consultants advising on educational pathways inside should be familiar with current eligibility rules and participating institutions in their jurisdiction.

Staying Current

The law governing plea practice, collateral consequences, and correctional policy changes regularly. Sentencing consultants should maintain subscriptions or monitoring in the following areas:

- State bar ethics opinions and rule changes affecting attorney-client communication obligations.
- First Step Act implementation updates from the Bureau of Prisons, available at bop.gov.
- State department of corrections policy changes affecting earned time, classification, and programming.
- Developments in second-look legislation and compassionate release provisions.

- Annual reports from The Sentencing Project and Prison Policy Initiative on systemic trends.

Appendix F—Consultant's Oath

The following oath is offered as a professional commitment for sentencing consultants beginning their practice. It is not a legal instrument, but a statement of values—a reminder, read at the start of each engagement, of why this work matters and what it demands.

The Sentencing Consultant's Oath

I will serve truth with empathy,

communicate with clarity,

and protect the dignity of every person I consult.

I will uphold confidentiality, objectivity, and respect —

ensuring that justice is not just administered, but understood.

I will stay within my lane, knowing my limits,

and refer without hesitation when the work requires more than I can give.

I will build the record that protects my clients,

support the attorneys who trust me,

and hold myself to a standard worthy of the stakes.

I enter every consultation room understanding

that the person across from me is facing the most consequential decision of their life.

I will not treat that lightly.

I am a sentencing consultant.

My work is both practical and sacred.

I will do it well.

Signed: ______________________________

Date: ______________

Name (print):

____

David R. Carrillo, MBA

Founder, David R. Carrillo Consulting, LLC

"The work of sentencing consultation is both practical and sacred. It requires intellect and empathy, structure and heart. Use these tools not just to build a profession, but to build understanding, one consultation at a time."

www.ingramcontent.com/pod-product-compliance
Lightning Source LLC
LaVergne TN
LVHW040514210926
848480LV00005BA/1457